# Avoiding the GREENER GRASS Syndrome

"This is an excellent book for all marriages. If you are struggling, it will give you solid steps to freedom, and if you have a good relationship, it will give you creative ways to make it great. Nancy is the perfect voice for today's readers. She is smart and funny, candid and caring, delivering an established biblical message in a contemporary package—I highly recommend this book."

—Bobbie Valentine
Former executive producer for Focus on the Family

"This book is wisdom born of tragic but genuine experience. Because Nancy Anderson nearly ruined her marriage due to infidelity, she truly knows the misery that a fling can cause. Her honesty, vulnerability, and repentance provide marital lessons guaranteed to revitalize and strengthen couples who are susceptible to the lure of an affair. Read this book and stay pure."

—Dr. Dennis E. Hensley
Author, *How to Stop Living for the Applause: Help for Women Who Need to Be Perfect*

"Nancy Anderson does a terrific job telling her compelling U-turn story of rebellion, repentance, and restoration. In the second part of the book, she gives helpful suggestions and candidly funny examples that demonstrate how to create a healthy and satisfying green-grass marriage. She has a delightful way of teaching without preaching. A must-read for every Christian couple!"

—Allison Gappa Bottke
Author/Speaker/Founder, The God Allows U-Turns Project

"*Avoiding the Greener Grass Syndrome* is practical, heartfelt, humorous, and motivating. Counselors and couples alike will greatly benefit from the honest insights of a couple who have 'been there.' If you want to grow a fulfilling, loving, lasting marriage, then read this book and buy several for those you love. It's right on target with a purposeful message."

—Marcus Bachmann, Ph.D.
Clinical family and marriage therapist
President, Bachmann and Associates Christian Counseling

"My husband and I have known Nancy and her wonderful parents for thirty years, so it's not surprising that Nancy has written such a wise and insightful book on marriage. She tells her dramatic story in a way that pierces the soul and provides hope for all marriages."

—Michele Bachmann
Minnesota State Senator

"*Avoiding the Greener Grass Syndrome* is an excellent guide for building, or rebuilding, a marriage upon the rock—Jesus. Nancy and her husband, Ron, have successfully rebuilt their own marriage by building six protective 'hedges' around it: hearing, encouraging, dating, guarding, educating, and satisfying. I recommend this book to anyone desiring to strengthen his or her marriage."

—Susan Titus Osborn
Author of twenty-eight books
Director, Christian Communicator Manuscript Critique Service

"*Avoiding the Greener Grass Syndrome* is by turns honest, humorous, moving, insightful, and practical. Nancy Anderson does a masterful job at telling her story without going into sordid details, yet remaining vulnerable enough to inspire and encourage struggling couples. I highly recommend this book!"

—Dena Dyer
Author, *Grace for the Race: Meditations for Busy Moms*
Coauthor, *The Groovy Chicks' Road Trip to Peace*

"Any marriage—whether brand new or slightly weathered—can benefit from Nancy's advice. She knows of what she speaks, and shares that insight with humor, conviction, and encouragement. This is a book pastors and counselors should keep on their bookshelves and gift-givers should bring to the wedding. Short of having Nancy as your very own over-the-fence neighbor, *Avoiding the Greener Grass Syndrome* is the best resource for solving all the lawn issues that can crop up in even the best of marriages."

—Shannon Woodward
Pastor's wife and author, *A Whisper in Winter*

# *Avoiding the* GREENER GRASS *Syndrome*

How to Grow Affair-Proof Hedges Around Your Marriage

NANCY C. ANDERSON

*Avoiding the Greener Grass Syndrome: How to Grow Affair-Proof Hedges Around Your Marriage*



Published by Kregel Publications, a division of Kregel, Inc., P.O. Box 2607, Grand Rapids, MI 49501.



Unless otherwise indicated, Scripture quotations are from the *New King James Version.* Copyright © 1979, 1980, 1982 by Thomas Nelson, Inc., Publishers.

Scripture quotations marked NIV are from the Holy Bible: New International Version®. Copyright © 1973, 1978, 1984 by the International Bible Society. Used by permission of Zondervan Publishing House. All rights reserved.

Scripture quotations marked LB are from *The Living Bible,* © 1971 by Tyndale House Publishers, Wheaton, Illinois. Used by permission.

Scripture quotations marked KJV are from the King James Version of the Holy Bible.

Scripture quotations marked NLT are from the *Holy Bible, New Living Translation,* © 1996. Used by permission of Tyndale House Publishers, Inc., Wheaton, Illinois 60189. All rights reserved.

In the first section, the story is true; however, some names and certain details were changed. In the second section, some anecdotes and stories have been changed or fictionalized to protect the identities of the persons involved.

Cover design: John M. Lucas

ISBN 0-8254-2013-x

Printed in the United States of America

05 06 07 08 / 5 4 3 2

*To my husband,*
*who loved me when I was unlovable.*

*To my parents,*
*who taught me when I was unteachable.*

*To my Savior,*
*who reached me when I was unreachable.*

# CONTENTS

# ACKNOWLEDGMENTS

*To God be the glory, for the things He has done!*

—ANDRAE CROUCH

This book was birthed with many midwives:

my husband, Ron, who is brave, steadfast, and cute;

my parents, Richard and Marion Alf, who are practically perfect in every way;

my son, Nick, who calls me Princess;

my best friend, Tonya Ruiz, who is Lucy to my Ethel, and her husband, Ron, who thinks we're amusing;

my pastor, Ron Wilkins, and his wife, Debbie, who talk and walk with Jesus;

my agent, Bruce Barbour, who is a gentleman and a scholar;

my first readers, Tonya, Ashley, Lindsay, Ange, and Juli, who generously strapped on their hip boots and waded though some really rough drafts;

my proofreaders, Kathy, Carol, and Lynda, who must have wondered if I typed this book with my feet;

my friends at Kregel Publications, Dave Hill, Dennis Hillman, Steve Barclift, Paulette Zubel, Sarah De Mey, Janyre Tromp, and Amy Stephansen, who are warm, gracious, and encouraging.

## Introduction

# Can a Marriage Survive an Affair? Yes, Mine Did!

Hello, my name is Nancy, and I am a cheater. I've never cheated on a tax return or a final exam, but I did cheat on my husband. That's why I'm an expert on infidelity—because I've lived it.

The "greener grass syndrome" has seduced many people into believing they'll find true joy and fulfillment on the other side of the marital fence. I believed that lie.

Ron was twenty-six and I was twenty-two when we got married in 1978. Both of us thought that it was the other person's job to "make me happy!" We soon found out that was impossible.

I complained and criticized my way through our first year, and then Ron retaliated with the "I'm a bad husband because you're a bad wife" defense. He was controlling, demanding, and impatient. We both looked for ways to punish each other, and our anger and resentment grew until they overshadowed our love.

That's when I met Jake. He thought I was beautiful, funny, and smart. He only saw the good in me, and he bathed me in compliments. We worked for the same company, so it was easy to spend time together. We started meeting for lunches, then dinners, and eventually—dessert.

So this book is different from other marriage books that are based upon theories, statistics, and clinical studies of infidelity: this book is about *real* life in the *real* world.

The truth is, marriage is both difficult and effortless, magnificent and excruciating, blissful and tedious. Sometimes it's all of those things within the same day—even within the same hour.

I know how hard it is to stay in a less-than-perfect marriage while TV talk shows and well-meaning friends are preaching the "you deserve to be happy" gospel. I looked for that verse in the Bible. Trust me—it's not there.

In the first section of this book, you'll read about the self-deception and lame excuses I resorted to for my unfaithfulness. You probably won't like me very much, and I'm okay with that, as long as you keep reading and give me a chance to show you what a swell gal I am now.

You'll also meet my mom and dad. My parents' "tough love" led Ron and me to reconciliation. Without their intervention, I don't know if we would have been able to see any hope for our future. Their prayers and insights led us to the door of forgiveness, and then we walked through it.

The second part of the book is about our recovery and the things we've learned in the past twenty-four years. We faced our faults, changed our behavior, and decided to love each other. The purpose of this book, then, is to give you hope and encouragement, and provide you with exciting ways to grow a fabulous, affair-proof marriage.

I want to show you how to grow the greenest grass in the universe—in your own back yard.

Your new friend,
Nancy

# Part 1

# THE ECSTASY AND THE AGONY OF MY AFFAIR

## *One*

# Betrayal

I was in love. I couldn't eat or sleep—I could barely breathe. As I sat near my desk at work, daydreaming about his kiss, he walked up behind me. I knew it was Jake before I saw him . . . his cologne. Polo.

He leaned over my shoulder and quickly whispered, "I made lunch for us. It's in a picnic basket in my car. I'll meet you at the Oak Street Park at noon." He hurried into his office.

*I can't wait,* I thought. *Oh no, I can't go! I'm supposed to have lunch with my husband!*

I called Ron and challenged him, "You don't *still* want to go to lunch do you?"

"What are you talking about?" he asked. "I thought we decided to meet at the deli? Don't you want to go?"

"It doesn't matter," I mumbled.

"What do you mean, it doesn't matter? If it doesn't matter to you, it doesn't matter to me. Just forget it!"

I heard a click and a dial tone, and I thought, *Oak Street Park, here I come!*

I left the office at ten minutes to twelve, driving with the windows down and the radio up. On the FM station, Barbra Streisand was singing "I Am a Woman in Love," and I knew just how she felt.

When I pulled into the parking lot, Jake was waiting for me. He had set a secluded picnic table, complete with crystal champagne glasses and white roses. He walked out to the car to greet me, and after a sweeping glance around the park, he kissed my cheek and playfully bit my neck as he whispered, "I'm hungry."

We sat side by side as we ate our fruit salad and drank the champagne.

"Have you told your wife about us yet?" I asked.

He nodded. "Last night, after the kids went to bed. It was awful. I felt so sorry for her. She couldn't stop crying."

"What did you tell her?"

"That I didn't love her anymore. That I was in love with you."

"Did you tell her my name?"

"Yes, and I told her that she'd met you at the company Christmas party. I said that you were wonderful, beautiful, and very smart. When I told her that you were very religious, she punched my arm, and said, 'If she's so religious, how come she's stealing my husband?'"

I winced. "Am I *stealing* you?"

"No, I'm stealing *you,*" he said. "Well . . . I guess we're stealing each other. I'm relieved that I told her. She wants me to move out. I guess I'll stay with my parents. Are you going to tell Ron tonight?"

"I suppose I'll have to. He's gonna freak out. He knows that I'm not happy with our marriage, but I don't think he suspects that I have a boyfriend."

Jake teased me as he sang, "Nancy's got a boyfriend; Nancy's got a boyfriend."

I laughed as I grabbed his tie, pulled him close. "I think you're flirting with me," I said, "and I'll give you forty-five minutes to stop it!"

He scrunched up his handsome face, squinted his bright blue eyes, and mischievously growled, "Set the timer."

Then he kissed me.

I left the park a few minutes before he did, and as I drove back to the office I pushed the radio buttons looking for a happy love song. I froze as I heard the voice of Reverend J. Vernon McGee say, "If you stop your sinful behavior, God will forgive you." I quickly turned off the radio and said, "But I don't *want* to stop!"

I went back to the office and called Ron.

"We need to talk," I said.

"I know. Where and when?" he asked.

"I'll be working late, but I'll be home at seven. See you then?"

"Fine."

After I arrived at our little condo, I hurried into the shower to wash off Jake's cologne, then changed clothes. Ron came in at about 7:30.

"You're late," I scolded.

He ignored my comment and asked, "What do you want to talk about?"

"I want to talk about us. We aren't getting along. We fight all the time, and you even hung up on me today. I think we need some time apart . . . to sort things out."

"What things?" he demanded. "Why can't we sort them out while we're together? You're so melodramatic. You always overreact. Why can't you just be normal?"

"Normal?" I yelled. "Do you think *you're* normal? You're the weirdest person I know. That's why I want to get away from you. You're too controlling and selfish. You never encourage me or compliment me."

"What's to compliment? You act like a crazy woman."

I shook my head. "You just don't see me, do you? There are other men who think I'm funny . . . smart . . . pretty, but you just insult me and try to control my life. Well, I'm sick of it, and that's why I'm leaving!"

He pointed his finger at me. "You are not going anywhere. Your parents will tell you to stay with me. We've only been married a few years. What about your wedding vows? What about the people at church?"

"Oh . . . so *now* you want to talk about church? We haven't been going for months, and you know why . . . because you didn't want to get your butt out of bed! So don't start being Joe Christian now. It's too late! Don't tell my parents anything yet . . . until we decide what we're going to do."

He softened and asked, "What *are* we going to do?"

"I don't know yet . . . but I know I need some space and time to think on my own. I found a little hotel near the office that rents rooms by the month. I want one month to sort out my feelings."

I escaped into the bedroom, shut the door, packed two suitcases, and walked back into the living room. Ron was sitting on the couch, crying. He begged me not to go. I stopped and stared at him. Showing no emotion, I walked out the front door.

After checking into the hotel, I went to my tiny room on the second floor. I knew I couldn't call Jake at his parents' house, so I cried myself to sleep, my tears an odd cocktail of guilt, loneliness, and exhilaration.

The next morning I put on a new red dress. Prancing into Jake's office, I closed the door. He looked up from his desk and said, "Wow, you look like a model. Spin around and let me look at you."

I turned slowly as I said, "I told him."

"Everything? Did you tell him about me?"

I continued, ignoring his question. "I moved out of the house and into a hotel. We can finally be together."

Later that afternoon, I told one of my divorced coworkers, "Hey, Carmen, I left my husband yesterday."

She said, "Good for you! I'm so proud of you! Life is too short to be unhappy. I love being single. Hey, I've got a great idea! Why don't you go dancing with me tonight?"

"I already have plans for tonight," I said, "but I'd love to go out with you on Friday."

"Great!" she replied. She touched my sleeve and said, "You should wear that dress . . . you'll get lots of attention."

I was tempted to call Ron to see if he was okay, but I didn't. He didn't call me, either.

Jake and I took separate cars to my hotel. As I drove past a church, I read their sign: "God wants you to make a U-turn." Anger and fear rushed through me as I hit the steering wheel and yelled, "Leave me alone, God!" But He didn't. I could still feel Him watching me—from a distance.

I met Jake in the parking lot, and he held my hand as we walked up the stairs. "Are you okay?" he asked. "You seem upset."

"I'm great," I lied. "Tell me how wonderful I am."

He cradled my face in his hands and said, "You are spectacular . . . glorious . . . magnificent, and I adore you! Now kiss me!" I melted into his arms, and we danced into the room.

He quickly hung the "Do Not Disturb" sign on the door knob. Then he locked the door.

---

## *Things to Think About*

Several signs may indicate that your spouse is having an affair. Which ones were evident in this chapter? The cheating spouse often

1. changes eating and sleeping patterns;
2. wears a different style of clothes;
3. starts arguments;
4. works longer or different hours;
5. pulls away from church and extended family;
6. takes more showers than usual;
7. compares his or her spouse to other people;
8. shows cold, emotionless behavior;
9. takes off his or her wedding ring.

---

## *Things to Do*

Ron and I should have done a number of things to improve our marriage. You can start doing some of them now.

1. Compliment each other.
2. Attend church together regularly.
3. Be honest about your feelings and disappointments.
4. If you're having problems, ask a trusted, mature Christian couple for help.

## Two

# Confession

One week later, Ron called me at work. "I want you to come home," he whispered. "My voice is hoarse from crying . . . please come back. I'm sorry I made you leave your keys to our condo. I don't *really* think you'd try to steal anything. Please come home. Can't we try to work it out?"

"You don't get it, do you? I asked for a month on my own. I've only been gone ten days. My answer is no. If I move back now, things would be better for a few days, but then we'd get in a fight. You'd swear at me and call me horrible names, and we'd be right back where we started. I need more time and so do you. Don't call me at work. I'll call you when I'm ready to talk."

His voice hardened. "How can you be such a cold . . . ? I don't even know you anymore. I wonder if I ever did!" Then I heard an angry slam and a dial tone.

Over the next few days, without Ron's calls to detour my thoughts, I fell deeper "in love" with Jake. Whenever our eyes met or he touched me, an electric charge went straight to my heart.

We still had to be careful when we were out in public, because I didn't want Ron—or anyone from work—to see us. So we continued to rendezvous in isolated parking lots and out-of-the-way restaurants.

One day as we sat in a back booth at a Chinese Restaurant, I said, "If I sell everything I own and make Ron buy me out of the condo,

I'll have enough to make a down payment on our cabin in the mountains."

Jake said, "I love to think about it . . . just the two of us. Let's get married as soon as our divorces are final. My wife said that she won't fight me on any of the terms. What does Ron say?"

"We haven't talked about any terms yet, but I'm pretty sure he'll fight me on everything. He's a jerk. We've fought about money from the day we got married, so I'm sure he'll try to make me suffer."

I knew that when I finally told Ron that I had a boyfriend, he'd go into a "this means war" mode. But I didn't tell Jake that part.

About two weeks after I moved out, I got a phone call from a girlfriend. Charlee Ann said, "Nancy, I've never seen a man cry as hard as Ron was crying yesterday. He's out of his mind with grief."

I felt bad because I didn't feel bad. I didn't feel anything about him. I just wished he'd go away. "I hope he can pull himself together soon," I said. "The sooner he accepts the facts, the better."

"What are the facts?" she asked. "He thinks it's a temporary separation, but it's permanent, isn't it."

"I think so," I said. "I can't imagine ever going back. I love my freedom."

"His friends at work think you must be seeing someone else. Women don't usually leave unless they have somewhere else to 'go' emotionally."

"I have several male friends who've been very supportive, but I'm living alone, in a hotel."

"Well . . . he asked me to call you to get a feel for where you're coming from. I'm going to tell him to start moving on because you're going to divorce him, aren't you?"

"I haven't filed any papers yet," I stalled, "but you can tell him that I'm looking for an apartment."

"Are you sure you know what you're doing? Don't you think you should go to a marriage counselor or your pastor before you do that? Can't you work it out?"

"I have worked it out. . . . I gotta go, good-bye."

One fear kept punching holes in my happy little cocoon; I'd have to tell my parents what I was doing. The previous week, I'd called my mother from my hotel so she wouldn't call the house. I just talked about the weather and asked about the Christian bookstore she was opening. Mother had a connection with the Lord that made me nervous. Even though I lived in California and she lived two thousand miles away in Minnesota, she was always praying for me. I was afraid she'd "know" that something was going on.

I went shopping for a place to live and paid a deposit on an apartment in Long Beach. It was tiny but cute. I fell in love with its cozy fireplace and charming pullout Murphy bed.

The next day I called Ron at work and said, "I need to get my keys to the condo."

He sounded hopeful as he said, "Does that mean you're moving back in?"

"No, I just want to get a few things. I rented an apartment."

"What do you mean you've rented an apartment?" His voice blasted into the phone. "I thought you just needed some time to think. I thought you were going to come home next week!"

"Well," I said calmly, "you thought wrong. I'm done thinking, and I've decided that I want out. I know you'll be at a convention this weekend, so just leave the key under the mat. Don't worry, I won't take anything valuable. I just want the dining room table, two chairs, and the couch. I don't want anything else from you, except half of our money and my freedom."

After a long silence, he said, "I'll leave the key. Good-bye, Nancy."

At my desk, I wrote Jake a note: *"I'll move into the apartment this weekend, and I'll file divorce papers on Monday. I love you!"* I walked to his office and stood in the doorway. He was talking on the phone, so I went in. I shut the door, walked around his desk, and rubbed his shoulders. He looked up at me and smiled. Winking at him, I dropped the note into his shirt pocket then walked out of the room backward—so I could watch him admiring me.

I knew that Jake had plans with his children for the evening, so I accepted a dinner invitation from my coworker, Olivia.

We sat in her kitchen, eating chicken burritos, chatting about her family's plans for the Fourth of July. Suddenly a wave of anxiety hit me. Hard. I felt a rush of frenzy and panic, and I couldn't focus my thoughts. The kitchen seemed to be getting smaller and hotter, and I couldn't get a deep breath. I stood up and stammered, "I've gotta . . . gotta . . . go." I went outside and sat down on the front steps. My whole body was shaking.

Olivia followed me and asked, "What's wrong?"

I whispered, "I don't know. I have to go. I'm sorry."

I drove away from her house, feeling like a magnet was pulling me back to the condo. I drove into the parking lot, saw that Ron's car was gone, and went to see if the key was under the mat. It was.

I walked in and saw the living room full of boxes. Ron had packed my things. I walked through each room and gathered items he'd missed. The phone rang.

I debated whether to answer it. *What if it's Ron? What if it's one of his friends? Or, worse yet, what if it's my mother?* I decided to ignore it, and the ringing eventually stopped. Then about thirty seconds later, it rang again. This time I picked it up and impatiently said, "Hello."

"Nancy?" Mom! My heart slammed into overdrive. "Is that you?" she asked.

"It's me, Mom."

"I've been calling all day . . . are you okay?"

"I'm fine."

"You've been on my mind all week . . . I can't sleep . . . I have a feeling that something's wrong. When I was praying for you this morning, I started crying."

"I'm fine, Mom. Just tired." I was surprised at how easy it was to lie to her. "I've been busy at work and Ron is out for the evening, so I'm here all alone."

"Well, I feel like something's wrong—wait a minute—your father just walked in the door. He wants to talk to you."

I thought, *I don't want to talk to him! He always knows when I'm lying.*

"Hello, Dolly Girl. How are you? Your mother's been keeping me up at night. She's worried about you. Are you okay?"

"Sure, Dad, I'm fine."

"I don't think you are. Your mother's usually right about these things. She thinks you're in trouble."

Since he already sensed that I was lying, I decided to let him in on part of my secret. "Well . . . Ron and I are having some problems. We fight a lot. He insults me and calls me horrible names . . . and last month we had a huge fight because I spent five dollars on a towel rack. He constantly compares me to his old girlfriend. He tries to control everything I do and say. He's mean to me, Daddy."

"Oh honey, I'm so sorry. So, your mother was right. Your marriage is in trouble. I wish we weren't so far away. Have you been going to church?"

"No, he won't go. None of his friends go to church either. I feel like he's a fraud, like our whole marriage is a fraud."

"How bad is it?"

I knew I was opening Pandora's Box, but since it had to be done eventually, I said, "I'm leaving him."

"What? When? Why didn't you tell us? Your mother's on the other extension. Tell us what's going on!"

"I moved out a couple of weeks ago. I've been staying in a motel, but I'm moving into an apartment this week. You were right, Mother, when you warned me not to marry him. He yells at me all the time and calls me filthy names, and I just can't take it anymore."

"Has he ever hit you?" Mother asked, sounding like she didn't want to know the answer.

"No."

"Has he ever cheated on you?"

"No, I don't think so."

"Why didn't you tell us, honey? We want to help you. But running away isn't the answer. Your wedding vows included 'for better and for worse.' Look, I know this is a terrible time for you. But if you and Ron will go to your pastor—or a Christian counselor—and do what they advise, I'm sure you can work it out."

The thought of giving up Jake was unbearable. "But, Mom," I said, "I don't want to work it out. I've already moved out, and I want to move on! I'm going to file divorce papers on Monday."

"No you're not!" Father commanded.

His forcefulness surprised me, so I changed my tactic. I found my "helpless little girl" voice and said, "But, Daddy, I'm so unhappy. Don't you want me to do what's best for me? Don't you want me to be happy?"

"Happiness has nothing to do with it! And stop trying to make me feel sorry for you. Our goal in raising you was not that you'd be happy, but that you'd behave. You've been lying to us for weeks, maybe months, and I think there's more to the story. I think you're responsible for at least half of the problem in your marriage."

He was getting too close to the truth, so I dodged again, lowered my voice, and tried to sound like I was going to cry. "I'm sorry, Daddy. I should have told you. I was afraid you'd yell at me or be mad."

"I am mad! You're acting like a selfish child, and we won't support you in this separation. The only way we'd ever support you is if you'd exhausted all possible ways to save your marriage. I have a feeling you haven't done one thing to build it up. I think you've been tearing it down with your own hands."

I started to cry. Real tears, this time.

They were both silent as they listened to my facade cracking. My father hadn't yelled at me since I got caught shoplifting when I was in junior high. I deserved it then and, deep inside, I knew I deserved it again.

My mother broke the silence. "Nancy, we love you. And because we love you, we will not support your leaving Ron. You are a Christian woman who went to five years of Bible college, and you know what God's Word says about marriage. It is a holy bond. Since Ron has not committed adultery, you have no biblical grounds to divorce him. You would be out of God's will if you did."

I hadn't thought about God's will in months. I started to panic, and the phone was slippery and hot in my hands. I couldn't bring myself to a full confession, but I did concede, "I haven't been a very good wife."

Dad gently said, "But that can change. Now that you've been honest about your own part in this mess, the Lord can heal your marriage if you ask Him to. Where's Ron right now?"

"He's at a convention. He won't be home for several hours."

"I want you to promise me something. Stay there until he gets home. Don't go back to your hotel tonight. Wait for him to come home. I want him to know that we'll help you both. We won't side with you . . . against him. We want you to stay married and fulfill the promises you made to each other . . . and to the Lord. Nancy, will you stay there and tell him what we said?"

I felt like I should do what he asked. "Yes, Daddy, I promise."

Mom said, "I think we should pray."

Dad agreed. "Dear Lord, King of Creation, we praise You and give glory to Your name. Thank You for the gift of our daughter. We love her with all our hearts, but You love her even more, Lord. Guide her to do Your will. Draw her to Your side and wrap Your loving arms around her. Lead her back into Your light. We come against any attacks of the Devil, and break any influences of evil in her life. Help her to confess her faults to Ron, and to You, Lord. Please help them both to put You back on the throne of their lives and their marriage. Let tonight be the turning point. In Jesus' name, amen."

Mother tearfully said, "Amen."

I'm sure they were waiting for me to say it too. But I knew that *amen* meant "Let it be so," and I wasn't sure I wanted what he'd prayed for. So I said, "Thank you, Daddy . . . Mom . . . I'll wait for Ron. I promise I won't leave until I talk to him. We'll call you in the morning. Good night." Then I hung up the phone—fast.

I looked at the clock on the television, 8:00 P.M. *Plenty of time,* I thought, *he won't be home until midnight.*

I didn't want to think about what I was going to tell him, so I decided to distract myself by packing some books. I grabbed an empty box, went into the office/guest room and sat down on the floor next to the bookshelf. I read the titles: *The Living Bible; I'm Ok You're Ok; My Utmost for His Highest; The Valley of the Dolls; How to Know God's Will.* I froze. . . . There it was again—God's will. I couldn't seem to get away from it. I felt like the questions were chasing me: "What is God's will for your life?" "Are you going to do it?" I decided to decide.

I went back to the living room, sank into the sofa, and held a pillow to my chest. I thought, *I could just leave and tell my parents that Ron didn't come home. No, they'd find out I was lying. I'm sick of lying. There's only one way out of this.* I took a deep breath and said aloud the words I'd been avoiding: "Okay, Lord, show me. . . ."

His holy power swept over me like a tidal wave, and I fell over onto the couch. I curled up in a fetal position to shield myself from His awesome strength. I was helpless . . . defenseless. I had no weapons except lies and selfishness, and they snapped like twigs against the sword of God's Word. Scriptures flew at me . . . they cut me and I bled. But I wasn't afraid because I knew that God was performing surgery on my soul.

> *I am the Lord your God . . . [and] you shall have no other gods before Me.*[1]

Hot tears singed my face and I answered in a voice that was broken and trembling, "I have been my own god."

> *Obey your parents in the Lord, for this is right.*[2]

"I've been disobedient and a liar."

> *Every wise woman builds her house,*
> *But the foolish pulls it down with her hands.*[3]

"I've ripped apart my own marriage."

> *If we confess our sins, He is faithful and just to forgive us our sins and to cleanse us from all unrighteousness.*[4]

"I'm filthy and unworthy. I confess my sins of adultery, selfishness, pride, deceit, and rebellion. Please wash me . . . forgive me. I know I'm not worthy of your love or forgiveness, but I surrender to your will."

Suddenly, I remembered what Jesus said to the woman caught in adultery; "*Neither do I condemn you; go and sin no more.*"[5] I knew exactly what I had to do. "Please, Lord, give me the strength to walk away from Jake and make a full confession to Ron. I want to follow you, Lord. Please help me save my marriage."

I closed my eyes and offered my thanks in hymns and praise songs. All the words had new meaning—and so did my life.

The sound of jangling keys and the bright light from the front porch interrupted my worship. I looked up to see Ron's silhouette in the doorway.

---

## *Things to Think About*

Ron and I had several serious problems in our marriage, even before I met Jake. Are any of these things present in your marriage?

1. Name-calling (using disrespectful or profane names)
2. Comparing your spouse to an ex-boyfriend or ex-girlfriend
3. Disagreeing more than you agree
4. Feeling unappreciated and undervalued
5. Resentful or controlling behaviors
6. Criticizing more than you compliment
7. Discounting your mate's needs as silly or unimportant
8. Hiding your true feelings
9. Lying about your behavior in order to avoid an argument

---

## *Things to Do*

If you have any of the symptoms listed above, here are important things to do.

1. Admit to each other that your marriage is in trouble.
2. Ask for God's divine direction as you seek wise biblical counseling.
3. Change *your* behavior first. If you want to see changes in your mate, he or she will want to see changes in you, too. You can't control your spouse, but you can control yourself.

*Three*

# RESTORATION

He stood silent in the shadows and took a quick breath. "I saw your car in the parking lot," he said. "Why are you here . . . in the dark?"

I steadied my voice and said, "I'm home. Your prodigal wife has come home."

Long pause. "Why?"

"Because I belong here . . . with you."

He turned on the light and inched toward me as if I were a stray pit bull. I could smell the fear—and the hope.

I patted the cushion next to me and said, "Sit down, I won't bite you."

His eyes narrowed, "Since when?"

"Since a few hours ago . . . when I surrendered."

"To whom?"

"To God . . . and to you . . . and to our marriage."

He sat down on the far end of the couch and said, "I want to believe you, but—" He swallowed hard and looked away.

"I don't blame you," I said, "I've been lying to you for months . . . about everything. But I want to confess it all. Do you want to hear it?"

"I'm not sure. But I do want to know one thing. Everyone thinks you have a boyfriend. Do you?"

"I did. But I don't anymore. I want both of us to call him in the morning and tell him that we're going to stay married. I'll tell him good-bye . . . forever. Even if you don't want me back, I know I'll never see him again. He's married. I'm married. It's wrong."

Ron looked at the floor and then at the front door. He picked a piece of lint off his jeans and dropped his forehead into his shaking hands. "Half of me wants to know everything . . . now, and the other half wants to know nothing . . . ever."

I touched his leg, and since he didn't pull away, I said, "I'll just start talking, and if you want me to stop, I will."

And we talked until the dawn crept into the room. He never raised his voice and I answered all his questions as gently as I could. It was an oddly—miraculously—peaceful conversation.

He told me why he came home early. "I was at the convention, watching a show, and I was fine . . . laughing and enjoying myself . . . when a feeling of loneliness washed over me and I started to cry. I couldn't stop. My friend Les asked if I was okay and I said, 'No. I have to go home.' Logically, I didn't think you'd be here because you hadn't been home in weeks . . . but somehow . . . I *knew* I should come here. We left in the middle of the show, and I cried all the way home.

"When he dropped me off and I saw your car, I knew that you were here and that everything would be all right. Then I opened the door and saw you . . . sitting there in the shadows. I could tell that you'd been crying, and I just knew that we'd stay together. I can't explain how . . . I just knew."

It was early morning as we drove down to the beach for breakfast. I was amazed at the freedom I felt. My secrets had kept me in a prison. The weight of my sins had dulled all my senses. Now—because of my confession—I was free to hear the teenage boys laughing as they raced down the street on their skateboards. I rolled down the car window and inhaled the sandy-salty ocean breeze. Everything seemed brighter—more vivid—like when Dorothy woke up in the Land of Oz and everything changed from black-and-white to color.

While we ate, I asked Ron for his advice on how to tell my boss that I was quitting. As soon as we finished breakfast, we went to a phone booth and Ron listened as I called the office.

"Hello, Mr. Adams, this is Nancy Anderson. What I have to tell you is going to be hard for you to hear, but it's going to be even harder for me to say."

"That sounds serious," he said. "Are you ill?"

"No, I'm fine, but . . . I'm afraid I'm going to have to quit my job. Jake and I have been having an affair—"

He interrupted, "We had our suspicions. But why do you have to quit?"

I knew that since my *feelings* for Jake had not changed, I wouldn't be strong enough to fight the temptation. I had to remove it. I told my boss, "I'm back together with my husband and I know that the only way our marriage will work is if I never see Jake again. I'm sorry to put you in this terrible position, but I can't come back."

Mr. Adams surprised me when he said, "You're doing the right thing. Don't worry about us. Your marriage is more important than any job could ever be. I'll mail you your last check and give your assignments to the other salespeople. You must not have told Jake yet. I just walked by his office and heard him whistling."

"No . . . he doesn't know yet. Can you transfer me to his desk?"

"Sure, Nancy. I hope things work out with your husband."

I said, "Thank you so much for your kindness to me over the years. You've been a wonderful boss. I'm so sorry. Good-bye."

I said a silent prayer as he connected me: *Oh God, please give me the right words.*

"Hello, this is Jake."

"Good morning . . . it's me."

"Well, hello, 'me.' Where are you?"

"I'm not coming in today. In fact, I'm not coming in . . . ever."

"What are you talking about?"

"I don't know how to tell you this, so I'll just say it." I spoke without taking a breath, as if it were one long sentence. "I'm back together with Ron, I can never see you again, I've already told Mr. Adams that I quit, Ron and I have decided to stay married, this is my final decision. I'm so sorry."

He raised his voice, "Slow down! How can you say that? What happened? How can you be so sure?"

"I'm absolutely sure. My decision to stay with Ron has nothing to do with my feelings for you. I still *feel* the same, but I made a promise . . . to God and Ron . . . that doesn't include an 'out' for my feelings. I've made a *decision* to stay married. I know this seems impossible to believe . . . but I hope you'll make the same decision. I'm so sorry. Ron is here with me, and he wants to talk to you. Okay?"

Jake didn't answer. As I repeated the question, he whispered, "I heard you. I just don't know what to say . . . I don't want to talk to him."

"Then just listen."

I handed the phone to Ron and he calmly said, "Nancy and I are getting back together, and I want to ask you . . . beg you . . . not to have any contact with her. We have a lot of work to do, and we need to start with a clean slate. That's why she quit her job, and that's why we're asking you not to call her or write to her." Ron's voice cracked as he continued. "Look, Jake . . . Nancy and I both want to stay married. Please . . . no contact. Do I have your word?"

I put my face next to Ron's so I could hear Jake's answer. "I don't really have a choice, do I? Okay, no contact. But please, let me say good-bye to her."

Ron's eyes were shiny with tears as he handed the phone to me. "He wants to say good-bye." I closed my eyes and held the receiver to my heart for a moment. I slowly lifted it to my mouth. "Jake, I'm so sorry to hurt you like this. . . . So sorry . . ."

"Are you sure this is what you want? I need to hear *you* say it."

"Yes. I want to stay with Ron." I couldn't control my emotions anymore, and I started to cry as I whispered, "Good-bye."

"Good-bye, Nancy. I love you."

I hung up the phone and fell into Ron's arms. I cried from the pain and the release and the frightened hope. Ron stood still at first, and then he started to sway with a comforting rocking motion. I burrowed my face into his chest and he held me with surprising tenderness. The familiar scent of his cologne brought back warm memories, and I felt a tiny ember reignite.

As we walked back to the car, we held hands—something we hadn't done in months. While we drove, we talked about what we should do next. Since he had the day off work, I asked, "Should we go to Disneyland?"

He got strangely quiet and asked, "Why did you say that? Why Disneyland?"

"I don't know. I just thought it would be fun. I know how much you like—"

He held up his hand—to silence me. He stared at the steering wheel. I waited. He finally said, "I guess this seems to be the day for confessing secrets. I have something to tell you. A few days ago, when I thought you were never coming back, I called my old girlfriend, Michelle, and made a date to meet her tomorrow . . . at Disneyland."

I turned my face toward the window. The sting of jealousy surprised me.

The thoughts ran like stampeding ponies through my head. *He's always loved her more than me. If I'd known that he'd called her, I wouldn't have come home. She's married . . . I thought she was supposed to be a Christian! What a . . .* I corralled my ponies, turned back toward Ron and asked, with a bit too much sarcasm, "Are you going to keep your date?"

"No." He pulled into a gas station and continued. "I think we should call her . . . right now . . . together. I have her phone number with me." He took a slip of paper out of his shirt pocket and said, "Come with me. I want you to hear what I tell her." We walked over to the pay phone, where he put in some change and dialed the number.

"Hello, Michelle, this is Ron. I'm going to have to break our date for tomorrow. Nancy and I are back together. . . . Yes, we're going to stay married. I'm sorry to tell you this way, but I won't be calling you again. I hope you understand . . . What? . . . I know, I'm sorry. Good-bye."

He hung up the phone and stared at it for a few seconds. "She started to cry when she said good-bye. I feel like such a jerk."

I touched his hand and said, "I know the feeling. I guess we deserve each other. We're the Jerk family."

We drove home and called my parents. I gave them a full and tearful confession about Jake, and then we told them that we decided to stay married. Ron asked if we could come back to Minnesota—to get their advice about how to start over. They were thrilled with our announcement and told us that they'd been in constant prayer for us.

Ron arranged for some time off work, and within a few days, we were on our way to Minnesota.

We arrived at my parents' house late in the evening. After a lot of hugs and a few tears, we went into their neat-as-a-pin family room. Ron and I sat on the couch, Mom and Dad each sat in their matching recliners. After the usual small talk about the flight and the bad airline food, Dad boldly spoke the unspoken. "What's your plan?"

Ron leaned forward and asked, "Plan? Plan for what?"

"The plan for your marriage. You two are going to have to figure out why your marriage fell apart . . . how to fix it . . . how to make sure it doesn't happen again."

Ron replied, "Well . . . I don't know if we need to do all that. Can't we just move on from here?"

"It doesn't work that way. If you rebuild a house on a cracked foundation, it might be all right for a while; might even feel solid and stable. But when the winds and storms, and the earthquakes come, the crack will split the house. And the Bible tells us that a house divided won't stand. Ron, if you don't replace the foundation of your marriage, it won't survive. The memory of Nancy's betrayal and the guilt you'll force her to carry will be unbearable . . . for both of you. I don't think you'll be able to move on until you, Ron, make one of the most important decisions you'll ever make."

"What decision is that?"

"Has Nancy told you she's sorry for what she's done?"

"Yes, she's apologized . . . several times."

"Did she ask you to forgive her?"

"No . . . not in those exact words."

Dad got out of his chair, walked across the room, and sat beside me on the couch. He wrapped his soft warm hand around my trembling fingers and said, "Your mother and I have loved you every minute of your life. We loved you when you were good, which was most of the time. But we also loved you when you lied, and when you stole, and when you slammed your bedroom door and screamed hateful things about us into your pillow. And we love you now. So the advice we're going to give you is full of love."

My voice quivered as I said, "I know, Daddy . . . Mom . . . I love you too. I want your help. We need your help."

Dad continued, "When you tell someone you're sorry, it's very different from asking for their forgiveness. Your 'sorry-ness' is *your* decision. But when you ask someone to forgive you, that's *their* decision. That's why people avoid asking forgiveness. It gives all the power to the other person."

I said, without meaning to say it aloud, "That's a scary thought."

Dad changed subjects. "I know you've had a long and difficult day, and I think we should all get to bed. But I want you to think and pray about what you'll do in the morning. Nancy, you have to decide if you're going to ask for Ron's forgiveness, and Ron has to decide if he's going to forgive you . . . or not."

Then he turned to Ron, who looked confused and apprehensive. "Ron, when you forgive someone, you make a choice . . . to banish the offense from your mind and your heart. Jesus said that after He forgives us, our sins are as far away as the East is from the West. In other words, they're pardoned. Not because we're *not* guilty, but because we *are.* Our pardon is undeserved . . . it's a gift to us from God. If you decide to pardon Nancy's sin against you, you can never use it as a weapon against her. And if you do make the choice to forgive her, God will give you the strength to start a new life together. But if you don't want to forgive her . . . if you want to hold on to the pain, and punish her, and keep her wound open . . . that will be your choice. But I don't think you'll stay married. Tomorrow morning, before we have breakfast, you'll each make a life-changing decision."

Then Mom, who'd been silently praying, said, "We love you, Ron, for the tenderness you have shown to Nancy. She has been a Christian a lot longer than you have, but she is the one who walked out of God's will. We want you to know that we will do whatever we can to encourage you and support your marriage. We realize that you do have biblical grounds to divorce her . . . but it all comes down to what you will do tomorrow."

Ron nodded and replied, "I have a lot to think about. . . . Good night."

He left the room and walked up the stairs—without looking at me.

I kissed Mom and Dad good night, waited for a few awkward moments at the bottom of the stairs, and went up to our room. The lights were out and he was lying on the bed with his back to the door. I washed my face, brushed my teeth, and silently got in bed beside him. Wondering.

In the morning, the warm aroma of coffee and the sound of muffled voices drifted up from the kitchen. I was alone in the bed and whispered a prayer into the pillow. "Lord, help me . . . help us."

After I dressed, I went downstairs. The three of them were sitting at the kitchen table, waiting for me. I felt like the adulterous woman wearing the Scarlet Letter on the way to her hanging. If Ron would not forgive me, the noose would tighten around my neck and the floor would drop away. I was completely at his mercy.

Ron said, without a smile, "Good morning."

I avoided eye contact and replied, "Good morning." I got a cup of coffee and sat directly across from Ron, with my parents on either side. I offered a forced smile and asked my dad, "How do we do this?"

"It's simple. If you've decided to ask Ron's forgiveness, tell him what you want to be forgiven for, and then . . . simply ask him the question. Then Ron will decide if he's going to forgive you. You ask . . . he answers. It's the simplest thing you two will ever do . . . and the hardest."

Dad glanced at Mom, she smiled and nodded, and then he turned toward me and asked, "Nancy?"

Ron had his head down, and I couldn't read his eyes. *What if I ask for mercy and he denies me? What am I going to do if he starts to lecture me or list off all my sins?*

He looked up and I saw the wide-eyed face of a frightened twelve-year-old boy. I spoke quickly, so I wouldn't lose the safety of the moment. "Ron, I've betrayed you, mentally, spiritually, and . . . physically. I've lied to you and deceived you. I have no defense, no excuses. I've sinned against God, and you, and I am at your mercy. Can you . . . will you . . . please forgive me?"

He leaned forward, never letting go of my eyes. The little boy was gone as my strong and confident husband said, "Nancy, we have both done . . . and said . . . terrible things to each other. Our marriage was a mess, in a million ways, and a lot of it was my fault. But I want to make a stand here . . . today . . . to change all that. You've betrayed me, but I choose to forgive you."

Our tears mixed with the river of divine love that flowed through the room. Our sorrow and shame were washed away. Our hearts were knit together—as one. We began again with a new, firm foundation.

---

## Things to Think About

Our marriage was restored because we chose to follow these steps to rebuild a healthy marriage. Do you need to do any of these things?

1. Stop running away from God—ask for His help.
2. Admit your faults to each other.
3. Ask for forgiveness—then forgive each other.
4. Cut off *all* contacts to inappropriate relationships.
5. Be fully accountable for time away from home.
6. Ask for instruction from wise counselors—then follow it.
7. Identify and abandon destructive behaviors.
8. Rebuild your marriage with mercy as a cornerstone.

---

## Things to Do

1. Make a list of people whom you know have had affairs, then list the consequences of their behavior.
2. Have an honest discussion about things that are temptations for you and make a plan to remove these temptations.
3. Look up the divorce rates on first marriages, second marriages, and third marriages. (Hint: The rates get higher with each remarriage.)

## Part 2

# PLANTING AND GROWING AFFAIR-PROOF HEDGES

# HEDGES?

*A man planted a vineyard and set a hedge around it.*

—MARK 12:1

Fast forward to 2004. Ron and I joyfully celebrated our twenty-sixth wedding anniversary. What a miracle!

In the last twenty-six years, we've traveled thousands of miles, emotionally and spiritually. We trekked through the desert of Hard Work and trudged up the slopes of Patience and Compromise. And, even though we often went for a swim in lake I'm a Jerk—You're a Jerk, I'm thrilled to report that Ron and I have arrived at the city of Deeply-and-Tenderly-in-Love.

## STEP ONE: LEARNING NEW INFORMATION

After we made the decision to reconcile and reform our marriage, we immediately sought advice from many different sources. We went to a Christian marriage counselor, who helped us learn to communicate more effectively. We also read several books about "starting over" and attended some marriage retreats and workshops. One of the most important things we did was join a wonderful church and faithfully attend worship services and adult Sunday school classes. We received solid biblical teaching from a godly pastor, and we acted on his instruction.

The transformation was a slow process. We'd developed many destructive habits, and some of them took years to die. We decided to stay together and act lovingly toward each other, and eventually our feelings caught up with our actions. We learned that married love is not a feeling. It is a decision, . . . and we decided to love each other.

About two years after we joined our church, the pastor asked to speak to us after the Sunday service. We thought we were in some kind of trouble, so we nervously waited in the hallway.

I whispered to Ron, "You must have done something to offend someone."

"Me? I think *you* gossiped one too many times, and somehow it got back to the person you were talking about . . . and now you're gonna get busted."

The pastor came bounding around the corner with a big smile on his face, so I relaxed a bit. But I was still mad at Ron for calling me a gossip. *How dare he!*

Ron smiled back at him, shook hands, and asked, "What's up? Are we in trouble?"

The pastor laughed and said, "No, quite the opposite. I want to offer a marriage enrichment class during the adult Sunday school hour, and I'd like the two of you to teach it."

"Are you sure you want *us* to teach it?" I asked. "We have a long way to go on our own marriage before we can tell anyone else what to do."

"That's why I think you'll be perfect for the job. There's no better way to learn something than to teach it. No one who goes to this church, including me, has a perfect marriage . . . but you've come such a long way since I met you. I think you're ready. I asked the Lord to show me who should do this, and I'm sure it's you."

Ron turned to me and said, "I think it would be fun. I'd like to give it a go. Okay with you, Nancy?"

I knew it was the right thing to do, and since both Ron and our wonderful pastor felt like we were up to the task, I sounded cautiously optimistic. But I was secretly terrified. "When do we start and what do we do?"

Our pastor said, "All you have to do is follow the written instructions in this book and go through the workbooks with your class." He handed us a teachers' manual and then he prayed a wonderful prayer full of blessings and encouragement.

## STEP TWO: TEACHING OTHERS

Teaching was a huge step for us, so we tried to do it perfectly, and that was a serious mistake. At first, we thought that we had to set a flawless example. We assumed that our students would only listen to us if we had a perfect marriage, so we didn't tell them about any of our problems. Our plan backfired because they were also reluctant to admit their faults. We all pretended that we were not human, so none of our marriages changed or grew. That's when we decided that the only way to get people to talk about *their* difficulties was to be totally transparent about ours.

We told our class of fifteen to twenty couples about my affair. We gave them the whole truth about the death and resurrection of our marriage. They were astonished that our lives had been such a mess!

Once Ron and I admitted that we still had fights—and asked the class's opinion about how we should resolve our issues—our students admitted that they were struggling too. They finally felt safe enough to be transparent with us, and that's when their marriages started to change.

We taught that class for twelve years, and we learned more than any of our students did. We attend a different church now, because we moved out of the area, but we're still in touch with several of those couples. They often tell us that those classes planted healthy seeds, which, in turn, grew the deep roots that held them together during the storms of their marriages. Later, we introduced the concept of affair-proof hedges in an article for a marriage column and, as we taught it to others, it grew into this book.

## STEP THREE: PUBLIC SPEAKING

In 1989, my parents asked us to tell our story to a Christian couples' group in Minnesota. I was so nervous, I was sure the audience could hear my heartbeat though the microphone. But Ron was confident that helping others was part of our healing process; and he was right, as usual. So we've been telling our story ever since. We're active in the couples' ministry at our own church and often speak at other churches' retreats, banquets, and marriage enrichment seminars. If any of Ron's tax clients mention that they're having marriage troubles, he usually tells them about our example of a "phoenix marriage." Remember the mythical bird? It burned itself up on a funeral pyre, then rose again out of its own ashes.

We've found that our story gives hope to couples who think that infidelity always equals divorce. We're living examples of flawed people who, with the flawless Lord's help, rebuilt our marriage from less than zero to 92.87 percent fabulous; there's always room for improvement!

The next section of the book contains some of what we've learned in the past twenty-four years of self-examination, Scripture study, and observations of couples who took our biblically-based advice—and those who did not.

## WHAT ARE HEDGES?

Since our reconciliation in 1980, we've completely rebuilt our marriage. We had to destroy the old foundation—selfishness—and rebuild upon the rock—Jesus. We used a perfect blueprint—the Bible—and now our home stands firm.

We also created a new landscape for our marriage, planting hedges around it for protection. What are hedges? Hedges are boundaries. In Mark 12:1 Jesus said, "A man planted a vineyard and set a hedge around it." First, the man planted a vineyard. Think of your marriage as a vineyard. You "planted" it the day you said, *I do.* Next, the man in the parable placed a hedge around his vineyard. Why? Several reasons: to *protect it from intrusion* by animals and thieves; to keep *his* vines inside *his* vineyard; and to *separate his territory* from his neighbor's. A hedge makes the statement, "Private Property, No Trespassing." The symbolic hedges around our marriages serve the same purposes. As a married couple, your goal, as co-owners of your vineyard, is to keep the good things in—and the bad things out. The HEDGES in the next six chapters consist of simple principles that will protect your marriage from external invaders and internal discontent. They consist of action words:

**H**earing: listening and speaking with patience and understanding;
**E**ncouraging: helping each other;
**D**ating: keeping it fresh and fun;
**G**uarding: agreeing on your boundaries—and enforcing them;
**E**ducating: becoming an expert on your mate;
**S**atisfying: meeting each other's needs.

Remember, these hedges must be watered, trimmed, and kept pest-free for the rest of your vineyard's life. That's where the hard work comes in. So put on your overalls and work boots, get your shovel, your hoe, and your clippers, and let's get "hedge'n."

## *Planting the Hedges*

Gardeners know that maintaining a hedge is an ongoing chore. But first, you've got to plant the hedge. And any gardener will tell you that when planting something, one of the most important considerations is the condition of the soil.

Assuming that Christ is the soil of your marriage, all the hedges, in order to grow to maturity, must be planted in Him. If you're married to a non-Christian, your hedges and your hearts may be divided, creating conflict about the location of boundaries for your marriage as well as large gaps in those boundaries. You'll need to be willing to find creative ways to maintain your Christian "soil" without discounting your mate's needs.

Another important consideration as you plant your hedges is positioning them with room to grow.

Last year we hired a "landscape architect," who charged twice as much as a gardener, to redesign our front yard. It hadn't been updated since the 1970s. So after he yanked everything out, he planted some scrawny hedges. Actually, his crew did the work; he just talked on his cell phone and drank iced mochas. The hedges were supposed to act as a fence to keep stray dogs and children off our lawn, but the individual bushes were about three feet apart.

I asked him, "How can those puny things give us any protection?"

He looked at me as if I was challenging his expertise, and with a condescending tone in his voice said, "Trust me; I know what I'm doing. If I plant them any closer, they'd fight for the same sun and water; they'd crowd each other out. They'd all die. They gotta have room to grow."

The same principle applies to your marriage hedges. Plant them with the knowledge that they will grow, change, and fill in as your marriage takes shape.

### *Watering the Hedges*

We're all responsible for watering our hedges. But to have enough water to offer our marriages, we must have our own reservoir to draw from.

The foremost kind of water is spiritual water, which we get from our relationship with the Lord, who is the Living Water (John 4:10–15). Over the years, Ron and I have gone through several devotionals together, and it's also vital to have a time to read the Bible and pray as a couple. But don't neglect your own, personal relationship with the Lord. In addition to regular church attendance with my family, I'm reading the *Two-Year Bible* on my own, and Ron is listening to a series of Christian teaching tapes in his car. We often share with each other the new things we've learned. Sometimes he tells me a story or gives me an example from one of the tapes, and he also likes to hear about my new insights.

In seeking spiritual water, let the Lord direct you. Ask Him to show you how to build your marriage into a strong reservoir full of deep Living Water.

The second way to water your relationship is with intellectual water: new information. Ron and I have many diverse interests and, while we do most of our activities together, we each have a few things we do alone. I'm a member of Toastmaster International, a wonderful group that trains public speakers, and I attend the weekly meeting at 6:30 A.M. so I don't cut into family time. When I come home, Ron usually asks, "How'd it go? Did you win any more ribbons?" Or "What were the speeches about?"

Ron plays basketball every Saturday morning with a group of men at a local college. When he gets home, I usually ask, "How did you play? Did you learn any new moves?" With my encouragement, he'll talk for twenty minutes and give a play-by-play description of the game.

Our teenage son, Nick, and I are on a bowling league, and Ron likes to hear about our scores and the funny things that happen during our games. He especially loved the story about me lofting the ball backward as my teammates screamed and scattered.

We both try to have new information to tell each other every day. But it wasn't always that way. When Nick was a toddler, I was at home most of the time and my days were so repetitive that I felt like I lived in the Bill Murray movie *Ground Hog Day.* I knew that Ron liked me to talk about something other than how many socks the dryer ate and how hard it is to get spaghetti sauce stains out of Tupperware. So I made it a point to have something new to tell him every day. I started reading the newspaper so we could talk about current events and joined a "Mommy and Me" class so I'd have stories from the "outside." In the process of these new activities, I formed new interests and he looked forward to hearing what I had to say—and so did I.

When we talk with couples who are having marriage troubles, one of them usually says, "I'm bored—our marriage just isn't very exciting anymore. All we ever do is talk about the kids and the bills and watch TV. I know everything my spouse is going to say before he [or she] says it. We're in a deep, predictable rut. I need some excitement!"

Can you guess where they go to get their thrills? Yep, outside the hedges. That's why it's important to have some outside interests to talk about. Have your own "well" of experience to draw from. Keep your relationship watered with new information—both spiritual insights and unique, interesting activities.

A marriage that is well watered will have deep roots and will withstand the storms of life. If your relationship is in a drought, however, and its roots are weak and shallow, then the wind and erosion—life's problems—will damage and eventually destroy your marriage.

### *Trimming the Hedges*

Ron and I have been married for twenty-six years, and our hedges look completely different than they did ten or fifteen years ago.

When Nick was born in 1985, we had to plant new "parenting hedges." Then we had to modify them when we discovered that Nick had several learning disabilities. All the things that affect our lives, affect our marriages. Don't be hesitant to trim your hedges as your lives change.

Just because you plant strong, healthy hedges today, doesn't mean that you won't have to replant or transplant them next year. If your husband loses his job, you have a baby, or one of you has a medical or emotional crisis, you will have to redesign your vineyard and move the hedges accordingly.

My parents are still an integral part of our marriage support system. They're both now in their seventies and, although they've had some serious health problems, they're still strong in the Lord. A few years ago they retired and moved near to us in California. It was a dramatic change for them, and they had to reposition some of their hedges, because new conflicts—weeds—popped up.

Now they're both involved in exciting new ventures. Dad distributes Bibles through The Gideons International and volunteers as a prison chaplain. Mom has been teaching other seniors about "Leaving a Legacy," and they work together to host Bible studies in their home. They are a great example of a couple who has adapted and grown with the changes of life.

### *Little Foxes*

I asked a good friend who was recently divorced, "When did you first notice that your marriage was in trouble?"

She replied, "Looking back, I see that it had been slowly crumbling away for years. It happened so gradually that I can't even tell you when we stopped having fun or when we stopped holding hands. He started spending more time at work, and I was relieved when he called to say he wouldn't be home for dinner. We didn't have huge fights, but we were both critical and impatient. He says that he 'fell out of love' because I didn't care about his needs."

"Do you think he *ever* loved you?" I asked.

"Oh, I know he did! When we first got married, we finished each other's sentences and almost read each other's minds. We used to share all our dreams and make wonderful plans for our future. . . . But the last few years, I got too busy with the kids and outside interests, and he poured himself into his career. Our marriage was just on auto pilot."

"Then how did it crash?" I asked.

"There was a woman at his office who, he says, was everything I wasn't—exciting, interesting, flirtatious, and encouraging—and he left me and our two children so he could be with her. There wasn't any one big thing that killed our love, just a million little things."

Her story is all too common. A verse in the Bible warns us about the small stuff: "The little foxes are ruining the vineyards" (Song 2:15 LB). Sometimes horrific tornadoes, like the death of a child or mental illness, intrude into our vineyards and ruin them. Perhaps they are flooded by physical or verbal abuse. But more likely, the little foxes of indifference, neglect, criticism, or score-keeping creep through the hedges and rob our vineyards of their fruit.

## OUR CHOICES HAVE CONSEQUENCES

Someone might tell you, "I didn't plan to have an affair . . . it just happened." They're not telling the truth. The Bible asks, "Can a man hold fire against his chest and not be burned?" (Prov. 6:27 LB). I literally flirted with disaster, bringing an inferno to my heart and home, and foolishly thinking that I would not be burned. My self-centered choices, however, charred my whole family and Jake's too. Each lie I told and each sin that I committed affected other people. I don't know if Jake and his family were reunited, but I pray that they were.

When our marriage fell apart, it happened through my taking one little step at a time. I made tiny choices that all added up to two huge choices. I had to choose between my husband and my boyfriend, and I had to choose between God's will and my own. Be warned that each emotional step you take will be either toward your spouse or away from him or her. Choose wisely.

## *Things to Think About*

1. What are you doing to spiritually water your marriage hedges?
2. Do you have any little foxes that have intruded into the vineyard and are gnawing at your vines?
3. Have there been any changes in your life that require new hedges?

## *Things to Do*

1. Ask your mate to participate in a short daily devotional with you. (*Our Daily Bread* is wonderful. For more information: www.rbc.org.) If he or she won't do it with you, do it by yourself.
2. Tell your spouse a new story about your childhood—something that will surprise him or her. Make it a happy surprise, not one that gets a "You did *what?*"
3. Get out of your rut. Give your mate a juicy ten-second kiss before you say good-bye tomorrow morning.

*Five*

# HEARING

*The hearing ear and the seeing eye,*
*The* LORD *has made both of them.*
—PROVERBS 20:12

Ron and I sat across the table from Luke, our longtime friend. He silently lifted his wine glass to signal the waitress that he wanted another Chardonnay.

I pleaded with him, "Can't you give your marriage more time? Why do you have to move out now?"

He leaned toward me and put his elbows on the table. "I'm too tired to stay," he said. "I can't even pretend anymore. I don't love Anna. I haven't for almost ten years. I'm done. I'm in love with someone else now. . . . Karen really understands me. We spend hours just talking. . . . I tell her all my secrets. I want to spend the rest of my life with her."

"Why didn't you tell Anna how miserable you were? She was blindsided when you told her you were leaving. She says that she thought your marriage was normal . . . healthy."

Luke slowly shook his head and looked out the window. "I tried to tell her . . . in a million ways . . . but she didn't hear me."

"I don't think you did. I think you wanted her to think everything was fine so she wouldn't be suspicious. You were telling all of your secrets to your mistress—not your wife!

"Did you ever ask Anna to go to counseling with you, or tell her that you were attracted to a woman at the office?"

"No."

"Did you ever tell her that you were feeling lonely, or unappreciated, or unloved?"

"Not until the day I moved out. But she should have known."

"She can't know what you don't tell her. She can't hear what you don't say!"

He shrugged, "Well, she knows now."

"Yes, but it's too late."

## TALK ABOUT IT

Many couples haven't communicated in years. Oh, they talk about the weather, the bills, and the children, but they never share their inner thoughts, fears, or disappointments. That's how some affairs begin—by having deep, meaningful conversations with the "other," and once an emotional connection is formed, a physical one usually follows.

This chapter, then, focuses on cultivating your intimacy-building communication skills. One of the most important hedges in your marriage is the ability to hear, that is, to communicate with and understand each other.

The simplest way to start a positive pattern is to stop a negative behavior. The first part of this chapter deals with some of the ways we slam the door on intimate conversations.

### *Nag-a-tive Communication*

I used to be a world-class, Olympic-gold-medal-winning nag. When we first got married, and even for several years after we got back together, I wanted to win every argument.

Then God taught me the Parable of the Coffee Filter, and I stopped—okay, cut *way* back—on my nagging.

One day my younger brother Dan witnessed me at my naggiest. "I'm going home!" he said. "Your bickering is making me crazy—it wears me out. Listening to you two argue is more painful than chewing on tinfoil!"

I defended our behavior. "Hey, it's not like we disagree about *everything*. Ron and I agree on all the major issues. We hardly ever fight about big stuff like where to go to church or who's a better driver [me]. We just disagree about the little stuff."

He sighed. "Well, I'm sick of hearing you go to war over where to put the towel rack, which TV shows to watch, or who did—or didn't—use a coaster. It's all dumb stuff. None of it will matter a year from now. I can tell that Ron is really mad by the way he stomped up the stairs. Why did you have to criticize the way he mowed the lawn? I know it wasn't perfect, but couldn't you just let it go?"

"No," I replied. "We're having company tomorrow, and I want the yard to be perfect. So I told him to fix it. Big deal! Anyway, I won, because he re-mowed it."

Dan shook his head, "If you keep this up, you may win the arguments, but lose your husband."

I slugged his arm. "Oh, stop being so melodramatic!"

After Dan left, I started to wonder if I was pushing Ron away with my criticism. I got my answer the next evening when Ron and I went out to dinner with some friends.

We hadn't seen them in several years, but we remembered Carl as being funny and outgoing. Now, though, he seemed quiet and looked exhausted. His wife, Beth, did most of the talking. She told us about her fabulous accomplishments, and bragged about her brilliant children who were sure to be future members of MENSA. She mentioned Carl only in order to criticize him.

After we ordered our dinner, she said, "Carl, I saw you flirting with that waitress!" (He wasn't.)

"Caarrrrlll," she whined, "can't you do anything right? You're holding your fork like a little kid!" (He was.)

When he mispronounced an item on the desert menu, she said, "No wonder you flunked out of college; you can't read!" She laughed so hard that she snorted, but she was the only one laughing.

Carl didn't even respond. He just looked at us with a blank stare and a face empty of emotion. Then he gave his shoulders a sad shrug. The rest of the evening was oppressive as she harangued and harassed him about almost everything he said or did. I felt myself cringing inwardly and wondered, *Is this how my brother feels when I criticize Ron?*

We said good-bye to Beth and Carl and left the restaurant in silence. When we got into the car, I spoke first. "Do I sound like her?"

"You're not *that* bad."

"How bad am I?"

"Pretty bad," he half whispered.

The next morning as I poured water into the coffee pot, I looked over at my "Devotions for Wives" calendar.

"The wise woman builds her house, but the foolish pulls it down with her hands" (Prov. 14:1). *Or with her mouth,* I thought.

"A nagging wife annoys like constant dripping" (Prov. 19:13 LB). *How can I stop this horrible pattern?*

"Put a guard over my mouth that I may not sin with it." *Oh Lord, show me how!*

As I carefully spooned the vanilla-nut decaf into the pot, I remembered the day I forgot the filter. The coffee was bitter and full of grounds. I had to throw it away.

I thought, *The coffee, without filtering, is like my coarse and bitter words.*

I prayed, "Oh, please, Lord, install a filter between my brain and my mouth. Help me to choose my words carefully. I want my speech to be smooth and mellow. Thank you for teaching me the Parable of the Coffee Filter. I won't forget it."

An hour later, Ron timidly asked, "What do you think about moving the couch over by the window? We'll be able to see the TV better."

My first thought was to tell him why that was a dumb idea. *The couch will fade if you put it in the sunlight, and besides, you already watch too much TV.* Instead of my usual hasty reply, I let the coarse thoughts drip through my newly installed filter and calmly said, "That might be a good idea. Let's try it for a few days and see if we like it. I'll help you move it."

He lifted his end of the sofa in stunned silence. Once we had it in place, he asked with concern, "Are you okay? Do you have a headache?"

I chuckled. "I'm great, honey, never better. Can I get you a cup of coffee?"

I'm happy to report that I still have the filter in place, although it occasionally springs a leak.

This "coffee filter" technique is also effective in other communication. It's especially valuable with telemarketers, traffic cops, and teenagers.

We would all be well on our way to happy marriages if we just applied Philippians 4:8 to include what we say to our spouses. Let me paraphrase: "Fix your thoughts on what is true, honorable, and right. *Speak* about things that are pure and lovely and admirable. *Speak* about things that are excellent and worthy of praise." If we, in the words of Jiminy Cricket, "accentuate the positive and eliminate the negative" in our speech, our homes would be more peaceful and inviting.

### *Are You My Mother?*

Let's face it. It's easier to criticize than to praise, and it's hard to keep our mouths shut when our mate makes a mistake. Ladies, if you want your husband to enjoy your company, remember this important truth: *You are not his mother.* It's not your job to correct him, especially about insignificant things.

We recently got a first-hand demonstration when we went to visit our neighbors. Ron asked them, "How was your vacation?"

Joe said, "It was a wonderful trip! We left early to avoid the heavy traffic."

Sally interrupted, "Well, it wasn't *that* early. It was 7:00. I remember because I looked at the clock. Did you look at the clock, Joe?"

"No, dear, I did not look at the clock. Anyway, it felt early to me. So we drove to this rustic little mom-and-pop restaurant in the mountains and had some of the best pancakes in the world."

"I can't believe you thought those were good pancakes! I thought they were lumpy and cold and too expensive."

"Okay, maybe they weren't so great, but I was hungry, so I liked them. By dinnertime, we made it all the way to the cabin. It's four hundred miles—"

"Actually, dear, it's four hundred-twenty-three miles. I looked at the odometer. Did you look at the odometer?"

"No, *dear,* I didn't." He sighed and continued, "I cooked up some juicy T-bone steaks for dinner and—"

"We had the steaks on Friday, not Thursday. I know because I had a headache on Friday and steaks always give me a headache."

"You're giving me a headache right now. And if you don't stop interrupting me and correcting me, I'm going to quit talking."

"I'm just trying to help you. I want you to get your facts right. Boy, you sure are grumpy."

Joe stood up, mumbled a good-bye, and clomped out of the room.

Sally said, "I don't know what's wrong with him. We haven't been getting along lately. He hardly ever talks to me anymore."

That's because she kept shutting him down. He was excited about telling us his story, but with each of her corrections, he lost enthusiasm, until he finally gave up.

If you tend to be a corrector, ask yourself, "Do I want to be right, or do I want to be loved?" The divorce courts are full of lonely people who were always right.

I'm not telling you that you should *never* correct each other. If someone has made a serious error, pull him or her aside and whisper, "You must have forgotten that Aunt Betty's new husband doesn't like to be called by her old husband's name." In general, however, unless the slip is a biggie, let it go.

I was leading a round-table discussion at a MOPS (Mothers of Preschoolers) group. One of the women said, "I'm so upset with my husband! Just before I left the house this morning, he was taking the laundry out of the dryer and was folding the towels all wrong! I've shown him how to do it a hundred times, but he never gets it right!"

I formed a "time-out T" with my hands and said, "Whoa Nellie, you're forgetting the big picture—he's *doing laundry!* My husband hasn't washed a load of towels since Nixon was president." I took a survey of the other women, and only one of them had a hubby who was laundry literate.

"You have a jewel of a husband!" I said. "Next time he's folding towels, no matter how crooked they are, I think you should give him a big kiss and a 'Thank you!'"

Do you remember the story of the boy who cried wolf? If we whine about every little thing, our spouses will tune us out. Then when something serious is troubling us, they won't hear us.

### *Less Is More*

Sometimes we women tend to overwhelm men with our words. Most husbands belong to the Joe Friday School of Conversation—"Just the facts, ma'am."

I remember an incident from my teenage years that illustrates my point. My girlfriend invited me to dinner at her house, and I was amazed at her mother's ability to talk about nothing . . . in excruciating detail. Her husband walked into the kitchen, greeted us, kissed his wife, and asked her, "What's for dinner?" A simple question, right? She started with a six-minute narrative about driving to the grocery store, which included such vital information as how many yellow cars she saw and a blow-by-blow account of how she found the perfect parking space. Then she talked for five minutes about the groceries—what she bought, why she bought it, how much each item cost, and what it used to cost in 1950. She eventually got around to answering his question, but by then, our dinner was dried out and shriveled up—and so were our ears.

Save your detailed description of "the perfect pedicure" for your girlfriend. I hope that she'll at least pretend to be interested. When you're talking to your husband, try to get to the point of your story before his eyes glaze over and roll up into his head.

### *Hint and Miss*

Another way I drove Ron crazy was to hint at something and then throw a fit because he didn't "get" the hint. One sunny day, for example, we were running errands, and as we drove by a Baskin Robbins ice cream store I said, "I love lemon sherbet."

He just kept driving. How dare he! I guess he didn't know that my hint meant, "Stop the car. I want some ice cream!"

My friend Tonya would have understood the hint and said, "Good idea. Let's get some!" But Ron was oblivious. He thought I meant just what I said . . . go figure.

Men rarely hint because they've learned to ask for what they want. If women would stop the "hint-speak" and ask for what we want, we'd be much more likely to get it.

*Room for Vent*

I tend to think aloud. I use my words to help me sort out my thoughts and decide how I feel about something. Sometimes I don't want a solution; I just want to "vent."

For some reason this makes Ron uncomfortable because he wants to fix it, forget it, and move on. I like to take a long hot bath in my problems before I even think about solving them.

I used to be shy, as well as insecure, about what people thought of me. I was almost friendless because I was waiting for a warm and wonderful woman to approach me with a sign on her forehead that read "Friend of Nancy's." She hadn't appeared, so I told Ron, "I'm lonely. I wish I had a girlfriend."

Ron, with the best of intentions, started to help me solve my problem. He gave me a lecture titled "Friendship 101": "The Bible says, 'In order to have a friend you must be a friend.' What have you done to be friendly?" Then he got out a legal pad and a wide-tipped Sharpie and wrote in block letters, "Nancy's Friendship Goals." Next, he started to draw a flow chart. He was befuddled when I started to cry and said, "I don't want a diagram. I want a friend!"

Now if I just want to vent, I tell Ron ahead of time. He's even learned to ask me, "Do you want my advice or just my ear?" What a guy. I think I'll keep him!

In case you're wondering, I've since "gotten over" myself, because I realized that no one is thinking about me; everyone is too busy thinking about themselves. And after I volunteered to work in our church's drama ministry, I met my best friend, Tonya.

### *Want to Please Me? Don't Tease Me!*

Many couples tease each other, and if you can keep it friendly, it might be fun. If, however, your humor is at someone else's expense, it's too costly. My husband is a funny guy. When we met, he was performing stand-up comedy in Los Angeles clubs like the Improv and the Comedy Store. He even took joke-writing classes from professional comedians like Steve Martin and had a one-on-one lesson from Bill Cosby.

He was always looking for a laugh. So when I ruined a meal or gained weight, he thought of it as new comedy material. I thought his comments were insulting and cruel. We had some of our biggest fights about his definition of humor. After I explained how much it hurt me, however, he stopped making my butt the butt of his jokes. He's still funny, and we often write comedy scripts for Christian plays. But we share the same rule: Cruel personal insults are not funny.

These changes didn't take place overnight. I think the issues related to teasing took several years to resolve. If I can see that Ron is making an effort, then I give him some room to fail occasionally. If I went "postal" on him each time he forgot, he'd get discouraged and stop trying. As you see your mate start to develop new positive patterns, encourage him or her. Notice when your spouse does it right and overlook an occasional slip.

## BE SPECIFIC—BE HEARD

A few years ago, I hit on a principle that's saved us from hundreds of misunderstandings.

One afternoon I was frantically cleaning the house for Nick's birthday party. Ron was sitting in the den reading the newspaper. "Will you please pick up those papers," I asked, "and sweep the front steps? They'll be here soon!"

"Uh . . ." he grunted, without looking up.

"I'll take that as a *yes*," I shouted as I sprinted up the steps to fix my hair and make-up.

Twenty-five minutes later, I came down the stairs, looked out the window, and saw a guest's car in the driveway. "They're here!"

I heard Ron bustling around in the den as he jumped up from his chair, shoved the papers into the wastebasket, and zipped to the front door with the broom. He was sweeping the steps as our guests walked up the sidewalk!

He had no idea why I was upset. Later, when our guests left, I said, "Why didn't you do what I asked you to do?"

He said, "I did!"

"But you did it when our company was in the driveway!"

"Yeah . . . so? You didn't say *when* to do it."

He was right—I didn't. I had the *expectation* that he'd do it as soon as I asked, but I wasn't specific on my timeframe. Here's a news flash: Your spouse can't read your mind.

Now I say, "Can you do this by 6:00?" or "Will you be able to have this done by Tuesday?" If he can't do it, he'll tell me, and then I can either do it myself or make other arrangements.

## GIMME A NUMBER

One of the simplest, and most effective, techniques of communication is the "Gimme a One to Ten" rating method. If you use this system you'll eliminate a billion—okay, I'm exaggerating—arguments.

Here's how it works: If your spouse asks you to do something and you don't want to do it, ask him or her for a one-to-ten rating on its importance. If your spouse tells you it's a nine or ten, make every possible effort to meet the need. But if your mate was making a casual request that rates a two or three, it's okay to say, "I'd rather not," or "How about a rain check?" or "I'd be happy to do that, but not now; how about next week?"

This can work on big issues too. If you enjoy your home in the city but your husband talks about living in the country, ask him to give that idea a number. Maybe it's only a wish, and he knows it's not practical (a three), or he might want to move next month (a ten). If you feel strongly about having another child, but your husband feels content with your small family, tell him, "This is a big deal for me—this is a ten!"

I was surprised to find out how much time I spent trying to please Ron by doing things that were "twos" while ignoring the "tens." If you meet each other's most important needs, you'll eliminate much of the resentment and frustration that could cause holes in your hedges.

## THE EYES HAVE IT

Many couples spend time together, but they don't look at each other. If you can't remember the last time you saw your mate's pupils, your marriage may be running low on intimacy.

Couples who are in love want to gaze into each other's eyes. Prolonged eye contact is one of the most powerful nonverbal ways we communicate interest in others. So if your spouse avoids looking at you, or you're uncomfortable looking back, you two may need to talk about and resolve some issues.

When we learn to communicate effectively and honestly, our verbal and our nonverbal messages will be the same: You are important to me. I want to know you and share myself with you.

---

### *Things to Think About*

1. Do I talk more than I listen?
2. Do I correct my mate's insignificant errors?
3. What are the "tens" in my life?
4. Do I avoid eye contact? If so, why?

---

### *Things to Do*

1. Pray and ask the Lord to install a filter between your brain and your mouth.
2. Write down this verse from *The Living Bible* and post it on your mirror or the refrigerator: "Fix your thoughts on what is true and good and right. Think [and speak] about things that are pure and lovely, and dwell on the fine, good things in others" (Phil. 4:8 LB).

3. Increase the amount of eye contact that you and your spouse have with each other. If it feels awkward or uncomfortable at first, don't stop; keep doing it until it feels more natural. Remember that loving feelings *follow* loving actions.

## *Six*

# ENCOURAGING

*So then, let us aim for harmony . . . and try to build each other up.*

—ROMANS 14:19 (NLT)

The word *encouragement,* literally translated from French, means to give someone else your courage. Courage, then, is like love—the more you give it away, the more you have.

Ladies, you may think that men have plenty of courage and they don't need any of ours—but you're wrong. I've made a discovery that will change the way you look at your strong, capable husband: Sometimes he still feels like a little boy.

When your hubby is rejected by a job interviewer who's half his age, he feels defeated. If he's told that his credit rating isn't good enough to get the low-rate car loan, he feels like a failure. He needs to be reassured that you still think he's wonderful, even if the rest of the world doesn't.

We all need to be encouraged. If you help your mate in the ways outlined in this chapter, your home and heart will be a safe haven, and you'll both look forward to being there—together.

When your spouse is upset about something, or feels frustrated or confused, you might ask, "How can I help?" Your mate will probably say, "I don't know." So my advice is, don't *ask* what you can do, *show* what you can do.

All the tools you need to encourage each other are spelled out in the word HELP.

**H**ands—doing
**E**ars—listening
**L**ips—speaking
**P**rayers—praying

## HELPING HANDS

In the years since my affair, Ron and I have had several major setbacks—*not* concerning infidelity, praise the Lord, but in almost every other area. Because we've learned to give each other our courage, we've weathered storms that might have drowned us. We had a financial crisis in the early 1990s. The California real estate prices went so low, they almost sank into the Pacific. We owned a vacant rental house that no one wanted to lease, and we watched our bank balance fall as our credit-card debt rose. We had some very lean years.

I learned to help with my hands by cutting back on luxuries like going to the car wash—I cleaned it myself—and instead of having my hair highlighted at the salon, I bought a kit at the beauty supply store. I also used my hands to clip grocery coupons so I could save money on home-cooked meals. My cooking is so awful, though, I think Ron would have preferred to just eat the coupons.

When Ron saw that I was doing things to help solve our problems, it made him feel like we were on the same team and encouraged him to persevere through that temporary setback.

Another way to use your hands to encourage is through touching. (No . . . not that kind of touching—wait until the "Satisfying" chapter.) I'm talking about a reassuring touch when you're driving in the car, sitting at church, or watching TV. Reach for your mate's hand when you're walking through a parking lot.

Men are human beings—trust me on that—and all humans need lots of contact with other humans. Women get to touch and cuddle with the kids, and girlfriends often hug each other, fix each other's hair, and sit close together. Men, however, rarely get any contact from other men. And when they do, they usually just make grunting noises and slap each other on the back. Not very tender.

One woman came to talk with me because her marriage was boring. She said, "I don't ever initiate a touch because he always thinks it's a sexual advance."

I told her, "He's probably starved for your touch and thinks the only way to get it is through sex. For the next week, touch him *more,* not less."

She looked at me as if I'd just told her to shoot herself in the foot. "He needs to get used to your touch again," I continued. "My advice is to hold his hand or kiss his cheek when you're somewhere you couldn't possibly have sex, like at a restaurant, in church, or at family gatherings."

"Okay," she agreed reluctantly. "I'll do it for one week, but you'd better be right." The next time I saw her she reported that they were both more affectionate and happier than they'd been in years.

## LISTENING EARS

Ron is a tax accountant, and during tax season—January through April 15—he works from 7 A.M. to 9 P.M. without a single day off. I've learned to listen to his hints about what would make his life easier. He even jokes that, for those months, I seem to turn into a magic genie. When he said, "I wish I could get my feet massaged while I'm sitting at my desk," I zipped over to the mall and bought a deluxe foot massager. (You didn't think *I* was going to crawl under his desk and rub his feet, did you?) When he said, "These shirts are so old, the cuffs are frayed," I had new shirts in his closet the next day.

I'm not saying I respond to *everything* he mentions, but I want to help him be as productive as possible. If I can make his life easier and less stressful during his "crunch time," I benefit too. He's grateful for my efforts, makes more money, and lives a longer, happier life. Then when I have a deadline I need to meet—like for this book—he's right there to "pay me back" by asking, "How can I help *you?*"

Sometimes, we women talk too much. Men generally talk less than women do and use up most of their "word quota" during the workday. So when it comes to word output, our husbands can't keep up with us, and they quit trying. Then we complain: "You never talk to me."

Try, as James 1:19 says, to "be quick to listen, slow to speak . . ." (NIV).

Men who have had affairs, often list "My wife just doesn't understand me" as the reason they went outside their marriage. The best way to understand our husbands is to listen to them when they do talk . . . when they talk about their childhood disappointments and triumphs, or their dreams about the future. Ask questions like, "What did you daydream about when you were a little boy?" or "What countries do you want to visit when we retire?" When we take the time to care about their answers, it shows that we care about *them.*

Just the other evening I asked Ron, "What was the first movie you ever saw in a theater?"

He thought about it for a minute, laughed aloud, and said, "Well, the first time I went to a theater I didn't see the movie; I just saw the bathroom."

I was afraid to ask, but I forged on. "What happened?"

"There was a theater a few doors down from our house in St. Louis, and one summer afternoon I went there with my friends Jimmy Joe and Skidmark."

I laughed, "Skidmark?"

"Trust me, you don't want to know how he got his nickname. The three of us tried to sneak into the theater because we didn't have any money, but the manager saw us lurking near the back door and told us to leave. We were mad at him, so we decided to pay him back. So we stood on our tiptoes, peeked into the open bathroom window, and threw in a stink bomb!"

Ron was laughing so hard at the memory that he had to stop to catch his breath.

I was horrified, but didn't let it show. "The three of us ran around to the front of the theater," he continued, "and laughed our heads off as we watched the people tumble out of the door, gasping for fresh air."

I was thrilled to see Ron so happy about reliving his childhood, so I said, "Tell me another story."

He told me several crazy tales about his unsupervised childhood, and some of the silly—and dangerous—things he did with his cousin

Larry. I've learned, through the years, not to interrupt him or be critical of his youthful tales of reckless antics. I just laugh, smile, nod, *and* listen.

Later that evening, when we were lying in bed, he held my hand and said, "You're a good wife." But I think he *really* meant, "You're a good listener."

## LIP SERVICE: THE POWER OF A COMPLIMENT

The Bible tells us to encourage each other—to build each other up (1 Thess. 5:11). One of the easiest ways to encourage someone is to give that person a sincere compliment. Last week I was in the bookstore at our church, chatting with one of the young girls who works there. She said, "You have beautiful skin; it looks flawless."

"Really?" I said. "This morning, I was plucking my eyebrows in a magnifying mirror more powerful than the Hubble telescope. I thought my pores looked like lunar craters."

She laughed and declared, "I think you look fabulous."

"Thank you, Amber." I grinned. "I'm on my way to get my picture taken and your kind words will give me confidence for the camera."

Compliments are like magnets. We're drawn to people who praise us. Criticism repels us and we try to avoid it. Are you drawing your mate in or pushing your mate away?

Men and women have affairs for many different reasons, but a common complaint of both sexes is the lack of praise and the abundance of criticism from their spouses. If a person at the office is quick to compliment and a person at home is quick to criticize, which one would you be attracted to?

Florence Littauer, in her book *After Every Wedding Comes a Marriage,* devoted a whole chapter to "The Other Woman."[1] She tells the female reader to imagine what the woman who's plotting to steal your husband might say to him. Compare that to what you say to him.

When my affair was in the early stages, it was all about compliments. I used to say things like, "Oh, Jake, you're so smart, I could listen to you talk all day." He would usually comment in some positive way about my appearance, "You light up a room when you walk in; you have such a beautiful smile." We were both so starved for positive reinforcement that we were "magnetized" to each other. I'm not excusing our behavior—it was wrong. The point is, there's power in a compliment.

Another excellent way to compliment your mate is to praise him or her in front of someone else. You'll get bonus points for this. Ron is proud that I'm a writer, and he often brags about my accomplishments in front of other people. "Did you know that my wife, the genius, has had another story published?"

I try to praise Ron in front of Nick. "Did you know that Dad passed a really hard test and now he's a Financial Planner? I'm proud of him, aren't you?"

Barb, an acquaintance, admits that the downfall of her marriage began with the constant flow of criticism through her mind and out of her mouth. She now feels that if she'd made a conscious decision to turn off the negative cycle, her husband wouldn't have chosen to find his solace in hours of peaceful conversations with the "other woman."

Sometimes, of course, you need to talk to each other about problems or shortcomings. But if your attitude is usually one of praise, your spouse will be more likely to accept your constructive criticism.

Remember the old saying: "You catch more flies with honey than with vinegar." I never understood why anyone would want to catch flies, but you get the point.

## THE POWER OF PRAYER

Sometimes there's no *physical* way to help someone bear his or her burdens. If a person's needs are spiritual, your assistance must be spiritual. And that's where Christian marriages have a tremendous advantage. We can call on the majestic power of the Creator of the universe to guide us.

My parents have been married for over fifty years, and every morning they pray together. They've prayed through the deaths of their parents, the breast cancer that invaded my mother's body, and the recent stroke that, for months, robbed my father of his vision and balance. The key word is praying *through*—not over or under or around, but through. Sometimes we have to go through the fire, but as Scripture promises, the fire will not consume us.

When we pray together as couples, we bring a sense of unity to our marriage that will not be easily shattered by difficulties.

Just as your personal prayer life is an indicator of your relationship with the Lord, the prayer life of a marriage is a strong indicator of the health of the whole relationship. Praying together is an intimate activity, and in order for it to be effective, it must be genuine and heartfelt. Ron grew up in a family that didn't pray together, so it was hard for him to understand how important it was to our relationship. Through the years, he's learned that his prayers nourish me, our marriage, and our relationship with God.

When Ron prays for me, I feel as if I'm covered by a velvety blanket of protection. Even though I still face problems and setbacks, his prayers shelter me from the sharpness of the pain.

In 1990, Ron and I faced the most painful and prayerful seven months of our lives. After an abnormal ultrasound during my second pregnancy, Ron and I went back to the hospital for the amniocentesis results. The doctor said, as if he were reading from a textbook, "Trisomy eighteen is a genetic disorder that always involves profound mental retardation and severe disfigurements." Then he said the words that still live inside a tiny pocket I keep zipped in my heart. "Your baby's condition is usually incompatible with life. Most women in your position, in order to spare themselves unnecessary anguish, just get an abortion. We can schedule yours for tomorrow morning."

I couldn't speak. I stopped breathing. I felt like I was drowning. I wanted to sink into the dark water and die. We left the office without a word.

We knew that this child was the one that God chose for us, and we began to fall in love with him. Ron laid his hands on my stomach almost every night and prayed for me to bear this unbearable burden through God's unfailing strength.

My mother said, "Try not to think about the future. Your baby is alive today, be alive with him. Treasure every moment."

Over the next few months, we talked to our baby, sang lullabies to him, and prayed for him. I gave him gentle massages through my skin. We knew we probably had to do our best parenting before he was born.

Four months later, we met little Timmy face-to-face. The nurse covered his fragile, twenty-ounce body with a soft blue blanket and matching cap. His heart monitor beeped an unsteady greeting as she handed him to us.

His beautiful little rosebud mouth surprised me. It was an oasis of perfection. We held our emotions in check, knowing we had to pour a lifetime of love into a minuscule cup. Ron and I took turns rocking him as we repeatedly told him, "We love you, Timmy." He never opened his eyes. His heartbeat got slower and slower—and then reluctantly stopped.

We introduced him to his heavenly Father as we prayed, "Lord, here is our son. Thank you for the gift of his precious life and for the privilege of being his parents. We release him into your healing arms."

Then we cried.

The Bible says that a three-stranded cord is not easily broken. The three of us—Jesus, Ron, and I—were braided together through prayer. As a result, our prayers bound us together during a tragedy that, had we not been Christians, might have destroyed us. Instead, our marriage was strengthened. The three-stranded cord that held us together that day has grown even stronger as we've embraced the power of prayer.

We've also faced another challenge that divides many couples: our son, Nick, has several learning disabilities and developmental delays. Ron thinks that I tend to baby him, and I often think Ron is too hard on him—and so we have conflicts. Nick is eighteen now, but since he'll probably never drive, or live alone, this issue is one we continually work on. We've learned to "agree to disagree" on several other issues as well and not let our opinions rule our emotions.

Every marriage has problems and conflicts, but don't be discouraged. Through prayer, God can give each of us His strength and comfort. He wants to build us up and encourage us as couples. You'll have the strength to face uncertain times if you ask for the guidance of your Certain Savior.

## HELP FORMULA

This principle of giving HELP with your **H**ands/**E**ars/**L**ips/**P**rayers applies to anyone who you want to encourage. Remember it when your friends, neighbors, or coworkers need your help to get through a difficult time.

---

### *Things to Think About*

1. Do I criticize more than I compliment?
2. What are some of my mate's wonderful qualities?
3. What are some things I can say to compliment my spouse?
4. Do I need to change how I usually deal with crisis?
5. What things might my spouse be discouraged or worried about?

---

### *Things to Do*

1. I will help with my hands by
2. I will help with my ears by listening to
3. I will help with my lips by praising my mate whenever
4. I will help by praying for

Seven

# DATING

*Let your fountain be blessed,*
*And rejoice with the wife [husband] of your youth.*
—PROVERBS 5:18

Ron and I met on a lovely autumn day in 1976. I was a tall, thin, twenty-year-old college girl wearing a short denim skirt and a perky Dorothy Hamill haircut. As I sat on a park bench reading Groucho Marx's autobiography, Ron walked by. He took one look at me and felt his heart dance (Ka-ching! Bling! Bling!). I was his type: young, cute, and best of all, I was reading a book about a comedian. His first words to me were, "Is that a funny book?"

I looked up, smiled, and said, "It's great! Listen to this brilliant joke." Then I read him a paragraph in my best Groucho voice.

His face lit up. His beautiful smile and perfect teeth impressed me. I moved over, so he sat down. We talked about everything and nothing for over an hour. Then we started dating.

Before every date, he made sure that he washed the car, took a shower, brushed his teeth, and put on cologne. He was always on time, greeted me with a minty-fresh kiss on the cheek, and often brought flowers. Sometimes he even brought a bouquet for my roommates. He was my knight in shining armor, and I was his fair maiden.

He planned our dates with military precision; knew the who, what, when, where, and why of every event. He'd tell me if the dress code was formal or casual. If we went to a party, he'd always stay by my side, attending to my every wish.

Once we were at an outdoor wedding where the wind was bitterly cold, so he covered me with his suit coat while he shivered in silence.

He would often surprise me with funny or sweet cards in the mail or drop a note into my purse for me to find later. One letter began, "My dearest maiden," and he signed it, "Your knight forever, Sir Ronald." He treated me like a princess, and I loved every minute of it!

In November of 1977, he took me back to the park bench where we met and magically produced a tiny blue-velvet box. He gallantly bent down on one knee and opened the box to reveal a sparkling diamond ring. His voice quivered with emotion as he said, "Nancy, I love you. Will you marry me?"

With tears of blissful joy, I gasped, "Absolutely!"

I had visions of our life together: seventy years full of laughter and romance in a kingdom full of love. The next month, he bought me a little starter-castle full of dreams.

Then we got married, and my Sir Lancelot became Sir-Belch-a-lot.

Overnight, he became a three-ring circus of noises. While he slept, his snores rumbled and tooted like a calliope. Every morning, he blew his nose, trumpeting like an elephant, and he sounded like a tiger hacking up a hairball as he spit in the shower.

Our romantic dating rituals went out the window and selfish complacency sneaked in the back door. I was as much to blame as he. I stopped many of the behaviors that initially attracted him to me, like being flirty, funny, and cuddly. I criticized and corrected him about insignificant things, and he pulled away from me emotionally. We stopped trying to please each other and got careless with each other's feelings. He wanted more sex and less nagging; I wanted more money and less noise. We lost our romantic spark, and our sense of adventure and fun. So I went looking for it—elsewhere.

A danger sign that may appear right before a divorce is apathy. If you have an apathetic marriage, you've stopped caring about meeting the needs of the other person. If you don't *want* to spend time together or be alone with each other, your marriage may be in deep trouble. BB King's song "The Thrill Is Gone" is often used to describe such a marriage. If your thrill is gone, here are some ways to get it back.

First, ask the Lord to help you examine your own heart. You may want to pray Psalm 139:23–24:

> Search me, O God, and know my heart;
> Try me, and know my anxieties;
> And see if there is any wicked way in me,
> And lead me in the way everlasting.

Are you pulling away emotionally? Physically? Spiritually? If you are, talk to your mate, confess your part in the distance between you, and tell him or her that you'd like to feel closer.

One of the most effective ways to get back on track is to behave as if you *were* on track. If you change your behavior, your feelings will follow. Some people object to this method, saying it's not genuine, they feel like they're putting on an act. We tell them to try it, however, even if it seems forced at first, because developing any new habit requires discipline. But the more you do it, the easier it gets.

Remember that married love is not a feeling—it's a decision. If you behave in a loving and caring way, your partner will, eventually, respond to that behavior. When Ron and I got back together, we didn't *feel* like we were in love, but we began to behave in loving ways, and loving feelings slowly followed. We started with simple things like saying *please* and *thank you*, then we moved up to small compliments like "You look nice in that color" and easy courtesies like holding the door for each other. The nicer we were to each other, the more we liked each other; the more we liked each other, the nicer we treated each other. We began a positive cycle of kindness that grew into love.

So if your marriage has lost its sense of joy and wonder, you can find it again. Don't live a "settled for" marriage. Begin today to make a change in your heart and in your actions, and soon your feelings will follow. Trust me.

## DATE YOUR MATE

When Ron and I reconciled, we knew that we had to recapture our initial excitement and delight. This chapter contains some ways to do that.

If you want to be in love, first you have to be "in like." To accomplish that, you need to spend time together, and a great way to be together is to go on dates. We've asked many troubled couples, "What do you two do for fun?" The husband usually says, "Nothing. Well . . . sex . . . sometimes." Then the wife will usually smack his arm and say, "HUN-eee, you're embarrassing me!"

Most couples, especially if they've been married for a while, get into a rut, and the longer you're married, the deeper the rut might get. Rut-dwellers usually just stay home and watch TV, sometimes in separate rooms. Then on special occasions, they might have dinner at the usual neighborhood burger barn or go see a movie at the local theater. But that's about as exotic as it gets. Booorrriinngg!

If you want to climb out of your rut and try new things, here are some easy-to-implement ideas to give you a boost. Think of the word DATES to stimulate the "creative dating" quadrant of your brain:

**D**elicious
**A**dventurous
**T**hematic
**E**ducational
**S**urprising

### *Delicious Dating*

They say the best way to a man's heart is through his stomach, but it's true for women too. Ron and I love to try new restaurants. Whether we discover a down-home barbecue-rib joint, a mom-and-pop pizza parlor, or a cozy little soup and salad café, we're trying something new—together. We have a book that lists restaurants by categories and price so, depending upon our mood and budget, we can have several choices. Sometimes I tell Ron to pick one, or he'll want me to choose, or we'll just pick one at random. If you're on a tight budget, you can always split an entrée and order an extra salad.

You can also have a date at home by making a meal together. If you have kids, make them some macaroni and cheese and send them to bed early. Then make a romantic or exotic dinner as a team. My cousin, Linda, loves to cook alongside her husband. They have a custom-built kitchen with twin sinks, double wide countertops, and two dishwashers. Good for them! She married a doctor, but even if you don't have the dough for a fancy kitchen, you can chop and sauté as a team. Ron and I once made an omelet together that turned into some sorry-looking scrambled eggs. But there's no right or wrong way to date while you dine, just do what you enjoy—together.

### *Adventurous Dating*

I just got a letter from my friends Daryl and Joyce, who were both in their forties when they got married. First time for both of them. They're what's known as DINKs—Double Income No Kids—so they have the time and money to spend on travel. Their letters are filled with adventures, like going skiing in Switzerland, hiking in Scotland, and scuba diving in Hawaii. If I sound jealous, it's because I am.

Most of us won't be able to do those exotic things. But there are ways to find adventures in our own neighborhoods and within our budgets.

Do something out of the ordinary; discover a new, exciting activity for both of you. Ron and I took a golf lesson once. We were both so awful, the golf pro was ashamed of us and asked us not to come back. Well . . . not really, but I'm sure he was thinking it. We had a wonderful time, however. I got the giggles because the golf-guy was so serious—and we were so ridiculously clumsy. But it was a great date because we still laugh about it twenty years later.

Look through the newspaper—together. Find the weirdest event—then go! You could choose a dog show, a chicken plucking competition, a poetry reading, or a watermelon seed-spitting contest. You might even find a new hobby.

If you have the time and money, go to a bed-and-breakfast instead of a hotel on your next vacation. Check out a book called *The Christian Bed and Breakfast Directory* that will give you all the info you'll need.[1] It's a wonderful way to meet other Christian couples and have a romantic and adventurous weekend.

Taking a new mode of transportation could also be a great new way to see the world, or your hometown. One year for our anniversary, we went for a ride in a horse-drawn carriage. I once borrowed a friend's red convertible, and we went for a sunset drive along the ocean shoreline. If you have the money for a special occasion, a limousine is a wonderfully romantic mode of getting from point A to point B. If you can't fit a limo into your budget, most bike shops will rent you a snazzy bicycle built for two.

The whole point of being adventurous is to do something new.

## *Thematic Dating*

If you want to have a special occasion date, build it around a theme.

A 50s date might include driving to a malt shop or diner while playing a "Hits of the 50s" CD in the car and, then, after you share a chocolate malt—two straws, please—rent a James Dean movie.

A western theme date might include chowing down at a rib joint, going horseback riding, or watching a Roy Roger's movie.

If you live in a larger city, you probably have ethnic neighborhoods called Little Italy or China Town. A German village lies less than a mile from our house, and Ron and I love to go there. We usually consume mass quantities of schinkenwurst and streusel, then waddle down the cobblestone streets and pretend we're on vacation in Düsseldorf.

Some other theme dates might include Hawaiian Paradise in Our Own Backyard or, if you haven't pulled weeds in a while, Jungle Adventure in Our Own Backyard. The man of the house would love a date night called Baseball Fever or, better yet, Touch Football!

## *Educational Dates*

Ron and I both love to go to art galleries. We found a whole street filled with small artist shops, and love to spend the afternoon browsing around and discussing what we like and don't like about various pieces.

If you don't like art, some museums are wonderful places to learn about history and science. Most men would enjoy a train museum, a history of hockey exhibit, or a classic auto display.

You could choose to get a more formal education together too.

Most cities and junior colleges offer a variety of adult evening classes, usually lasting only a few weeks and having low tuition costs. The two of you might want to take a class in photography, computer skills, or gardening.

Most churches offer Bible study courses. If you take one together and do your homework together, your spiritual relationship will grow along with your emotional and educational connection.

If you learn new things as a team, you'll have completely new topics of conversation. These educational experiences will help you climb another rung on the ladder out of your rut.

### *Surprising Dates*

One of the differences between newlyweds and "oldlyweds" is that people who've been married for a long time usually stop surprising each other. It's not that they can't do it; often they just get lazy. But you can change that.

If you know that your mate would love to go to a certain event or concert, surprise him or her with tickets. Ron knows that, as a teenager, I had a megacrush on Paul McCartney, so he bought two tickets for his concert as a surprise. Wow, did he get a big reward for that—Ron, I mean, not Paul!

You could also plan a less expensive "mystery night." Make all the arrangements, then call your date and say to him or her, "Meet me on the corner of Fifth and Main at six o'clock."

Ladies, you could plan a free surprise by calling your husband just as he's leaving work, and whispering, "I'm cold and lonely, come home and warm me up!" After he breaks all the speed limits and arrives home in half the usual time, greet him with a kid-free house, a warm backrub, and a hot bath. It won't cost you anything except your time and attention, and those are the most valuable things you have to offer.

## LAME EXCUSES

When marriages are troubled, it's often because couples have stopped spending time alone together. We ask them, "Why don't you have a date night?" They usually have some combination of the following excuses:

- Lack of money
- Lack of time
- Lack of a baby-sitter

Here are some imaginative, clever, and practical rebuttals to those lame excuses.

### *Cheap Dates*

If you live in a city big enough to have a newspaper, you have access to lots of free activities. In the summer, free concerts might be offered in parks. You can raid your refrigerator, pack a picnic basket, grab a blanket, and watch the sunset with your sweetie—for free. Look in the community section for inexpensive festivals, fairs, and plays. Our local college, for instance, has a "Classic Movie Night" that costs a dollar.

If you both like to read, you could go to a library or a bookstore/coffeehouse and browse to your heart's content. Or how about a walk (hand holding required) around a lake. If you have a dog, walk it together. It's good exercise, and you'll have a chance to talk without the TV blaring or a phone ringing.

If you do a little research, you can find all sorts of coupons for things you like to do. I used to work for a company that sold booklets containing restaurant and event coupons. (For more information, visit their Web site at www.entertainment.com to see if they have one for your city.) Most of the offers were buy-one-get-one-free deals, and if you don't order a soft drink or dessert, you can often dine out cheaper than you could eat at home.

When Tom and Rhonda were newlyweds and didn't even have enough money for a discounted meal, they drove to the airport, parked close to the runway, and laid on the hood of the car so they could watch the planes take off. They have great memories of the "good ol'days—when we were poor."

My parents often tell us about their Friday night ritual of "going on a safari for loose change." They'd hunt through the house, calling out, "I found a nickel in my gray coat pocket!" or "I hit the jackpot! I found a dime under the sofa!" Then, when they'd gathered thirty-five cents, they'd walk to the corner soda fountain to buy two double-decker ice cream cones. They got married in 1949 so, allowing for inflation, today you'll need to find about $35.00.

Ron and I started to reconnect through simple acts like going for walks and visiting art museums. We'd take turns planning our dates, and each of us tried to choose something that would please the other. We agreed to talk about only pleasant topics while we were out because if we talked about our "hot spots" we'd start a fire and ruin the date. Lo and behold, we started to enjoy each other's company again.

### *Making Time*

We all have time to do what we want to do. The same couples who say they can't squeeze in a date night usually have plenty of time for TV and sports or shopping and talking on the phone. Dating is a matter of priorities and, other than your relationship with the Lord, your relationship with your spouse is supposed to be number one on the list.

But hobbies, television, work, and same-sex friends often take priority over our mates. If your "me" time is crowding out your "we" time, your marriage might be in danger. Ron and I were so focused on ourselves that we lost sight of each other. We had to make a conscious decision to make time to be together.

Planning is vital if your life is hectic—and whose isn't? We enter all our special occasions, like birthdays and anniversaries, on our master calendar in the kitchen and try to keep them as special one-on-one dates. We both like to go to plays and concerts, so we'll often buy tickets in advance. We write those events down too. And when we combine the plan-ahead dates with the spontaneous "let's go bowling" ones, we spend a lot of time together.

One of the most romantic things we've ever done was combine two activities in a time-saving way. We got our exercise and went on a date at the same time when we took weekly ballroom dancing lessons. It was very romantic because dancing requires intense eye and body contact. It also taught us about working together as a team and learning to trust each other, because when dancing, the man must be a strong leader and the woman must learn to follow.

### *The Baby-sitter Blues*

I sympathize with the baby-sitter drought, but you can't let it keep you from your mission of a happy marriage. You need some time away from the kids, and here are some innovative ways to get it.

First, do a trade-out with another couple. When Nick was little, we had some friends with a little girl about the same age, and we'd often watch their baby on Friday night in exchange for them watching Nick on Saturday. The kids were thrilled to have a pal, and we were delighted to be able to eat a meal—uninterrupted.

This arrangement won't always work if you have a plethora of children and your friends, with the white carpet, have only one. So here's another idea. Your best natural resources for free baby-sitting are your relatives—but like all ecosystems, you have to keep it in balance. Ron's parents or his sister, Jo Ann, watched Nick quite often, but we were careful not to overuse their generosity. If you suck the life out of your family, they'll quit baby-sitting. So use this option sparingly.

If no teenagers or grandma types are willing to baby-sit, you can still have alone time. When Nick was younger, we'd try to wear him out during the day, so he'd go to bed early at night. Then we could have a date in our own house. Sometimes I'd make a special candlelit dinner, and then we'd lay a quilt on the floor and snuggle up to watch a romantic movie.

You can also put the kids in their jammies, strap them in the car seat, and drive around until they doze off. Then, go for a romantic moonlit ride.

You can have a date during the day too. We used to put Nick in a stroller, and Ron and I would hold hands while we explored farmers' markets and antique fairs.

The baby-sitter problem is easy to solve if you're willing to be creative. And taking the kids along on some of your dates can be a good thing; kids are reassured, knowing that their parents like each other. They'll be more secure and stable if they see the two of you being playful and affectionate.

## DOUBLE DATES

Going out with other Christian couples can be another fun way to date. Have a short test-date by asking another couple to go out for lunch with you after church or inviting your neighbors over for coffee. If you "click" with them, you can plan a longer date.

Choose a couple whose family is similar to yours—kids, interests, same general income—and you'll probably find that you have a lot in common. We've dated with several couples on a regular basis, and we've been friends with some of them for thirty years. And seeing other couples react to each other and solve their conflicts has helped us to work out our own problems. It's reassuring, too, to know that we're not alone in having conflicts. We couples often ask each other's opinions about various issues because the Bible says there is wisdom in a multitude of wise counselors.

If you've gone out on a few double dates with a couple, and you think you've found a good match, the next step is to take a vacation with them. We've traveled with another family to the ocean, the river, the mountains, and the desert. Our next goal is to go on a cruise. Hey, I can dream, can't I?

Other couples also can keep you accountable. I know that if Ron and I started pulling away from each other or acting strangely around our friends, they'd care enough to confront us and try to help get us back on track.

Remember all of this rekindling takes time and patience. Take it slow, and if you're sincere about wanting to please each other, you'll both feel much better about your relationship. All that's necessary for a date to be great is the two of you being together, creating a happy memory.

## Things to Think About

1. What did you do before you were married that you don't do now? (Beside kissing until your lips went numb.)
2. If money were no object, what would you do on an ideal date?
3. When was the last time you and your spouse did something adventurous or surprising?

## Things to Do

1. If you don't have a master calendar for all your family's activities, buy one. If you already have one, choose a date night for next week, write it on your calendar, and draw a big red heart around the day. Next, plan your adventure—together.
2. Buy a Sunday newspaper and clip out a coupon for a new eatery, go on a loose-change-safari, and get out of your restaurant rut.
3. Call another couple and set up a double date for coffee or dessert.

# Eight

# Guarding

*Above all else, guard your heart, for it affects everything you do.*

—PROVERBS 4:23 (NLT)

When Secret Service agents guard the president, they continually scan the crowd. They're looking for unusual movements or odd behaviors that may be an indication of danger. The agents have studied how innocent people usually behave, so they can spot a person who's acting "guilty." We can apply some of these lessons to guarding our marriages.

You don't need to be paranoid or to see things that aren't there. I don't recommend that you spy on your spouse . . . but if you need to, feel free. It would be wise, however, to be on guard.

Kate's husband divorced her—she didn't even see it coming. She told me, "My gut was telling me that things weren't quite right, but I thought I was just being too sensitive. I talked myself out of my suspicions."

I asked her, "Could you make a list of his unusual behaviors? Things that weren't bad—just odd. And now, looking back, you see them as signs that he was having an affair.

Here is Kate's top-ten list:

1. He used to sit and watch TV with me or play games with the kids in the evenings. But about six months ago he started working longer hours and having more "client dinners."

2. When he was home, he would often have "work" to do, so he spent a lot of time in the den—with the door closed.
3. He started doing new things that, at the time, I thought were wonderful. He took the dog for long walks, and offered to run errands for me in the evenings. If I commented that I wished I had some cookies for the kids' lunches, he'd say, "I'll be happy to run to the store for you." I found out later that he'd call his mistress on his cell phone while he was walking or running errands.
4. He gave me a goofy, silly card for my birthday instead of his usual romantic, sentimental one, and he only signed his name—not "Love, Bob."
5. Our sex life diminished. On the rare occasion when we did make love, it felt awkwardly cold—just a physical act, not an emotional connection. He may have felt as if he was being unfaithful to his girlfriend by sleeping with me.
6. He started referring to a person at work named Pierce. He would tell me how funny and talented Pierce was. That was his mistress's *last* name!
7. He started to skip desserts and be very careful about what he ate—he lost weight.
8. He dyed his hair and mustache to cover the gray. "She" is twelve years younger than he.
9. He seemed more short-tempered. Things that didn't usually bother him, suddenly did. He was especially impatient with the children.
10. After I saw the way he reacted to "her" at a company party, I asked him if there was something between them, and he lied to my face. I knew he was lying, but by then it was too late. Looking back, I know he lied to me about credit card and cell phone bills, and that most of the new clients he'd been taking to dinner were not clients at all.

Kate summed it all up: "I wish I'd been more alert. I just didn't put all the pieces together until it was too late."

When you're guarding your marriage, you're not guarding just your spouse, but guarding yourself too. I rationalized my way into a boatload of trouble because I thought, *The rules don't apply to me. I've been to Bible College, I'm smart, I have self-control, and I can stop before it gets too far.* All lies!

The guarding hedges are as much for you as they are for your mate. We're all bombarded with suggestive commercials and invitations to sin. If you don't think so, just turn on your television. On second thought—don't.

Affairs begin in many ways and for many reasons, so we must be always on guard for the slightest hint of temptation. Because hints turn into flirtations, flirtations turn into attractions, attractions turn into affairs, and affairs turn into disasters. First Corinthians 10:13 says that God will always provide a way of escape, but we have to make a decision to run toward the door.

## PLANTING HEDGES

The subtitle of this book, *How to Grow Affair-Proof Hedges Around Your Marriage,* refers to the safeguards that you can "plant" around your marriage. Some of your hedges will grow and change as your marriage goes through different stages, but here are some of the areas where guarding hedges will protect you.

### *In the Workplace*

My affair began at work, so I'm an expert on workplace temptation. Once, the most common type of office infidelity was between male bosses and females who were lower-ranking employees, but that's changed in the last ten years. With more and more women working, the most common office affair is between coworkers.

Jake was not my boss; we were both sales reps—equals.

Coworkers sometimes work on projects or solve problems together, and the resulting closeness can build teamwork—but it can also build a feeling of intimacy. If you feel an attraction to someone in your office, consider a transfer to a different department, a different position, or maybe you should quit. No job is more valuable than your marriage. I knew that I could not continue to work with Jake without being tempted, so I had to choose to give all or nothing, and I chose to give all—to my marriage.

Be honest with yourself. If you're dressing to please someone at work or lingering in the parking lot hoping that person will ask you to lunch, stop now, before you've gone too far.

If you're in doubt as to what conduct is inappropriate, ask yourself, *Would I do this in front of my spouse?* And if you're still not sure, ask yourself, *Would I do it in front of the Lord?* (You are, you know.) Here is a simple rule to keep you on the straight and narrow: If you'd have to hide it or lie about it—don't do it!

My relationship with Jake started innocently. I noticed that he laughed at the same things I laughed at, and he noticed that we both liked similar music, so we started to sit together in the lunchroom. We were just friends . . . until we weren't.

I remember the first time we went out of the friendship zone and into the danger zone. We were sitting next to each other at a sales meeting when his leg brushed up against mine. I felt a spark at the contact point and was a bit disappointed when he pulled away. A few minutes later, he shifted slightly in his chair and his leg, from knee to thigh, pressed gently against mine. I liked it, and I didn't pull away.

I should have. And because I didn't, I sent him a signal that I was unguarded. We both began to look for excuses to be together. If I'd pulled away and not responded to his flirtations, I would have avoided the biggest regret of my life.

Many Christian companies have codes of conduct that are safeguards against the temptations of emotional or physical affairs with coworkers. Here are some suggestions to keep you out of the danger zone:

1. People of the opposite sex should not ride in a car together without a third party present.
2. Don't make personal phone calls to another employee of the opposite sex.
3. Don't have lunch with the same person every day. Move around the lunchroom, and if you go out to a restaurant, go in a group.

4. Make sure that your e-mails and other correspondence are not suggestive, inappropriate, or flirtatious.
5. Talk about your spouse in positive terms, making it clear that you're married and intend to stay that way.
6. Be careful not to make any lingering eye contact.
7. The only appropriate touch between business associates of the opposite sex is a handshake.

Here are a few guarding hedges to plant around your business travel:

1. If your job requires traveling with another employee of the opposite sex, do not get adjoining hotel rooms. If possible, request a room on a different floor.
2. If you have to meet with that person, offer to get together in the coffee shop or the lobby.
3. Call your spouse every night at a designated time and give him or her full permission to call your cell phone—anytime.
4. Ask the hotel clerk to block out all adult TV channels.

Discuss these lists with your spouse and add any other things you feel are necessary. Then, give your mate permission to correct you if you go out-of-bounds.

According to one newspaper article, working with people of the opposite sex can be hazardous to your marriage.[1] If you, as a woman, worked with all women, your chances for a divorce would be much lower than if you worked with mostly men. If, however, you're a married woman and you work with mostly single or newly divorced females, your divorce risk is much higher than if your coworkers were married. In other words, divorce can be contagious.

If you're in a workplace that's a landmine of temptation or if many of your coworkers are swingin' singles, be on guard.

Many years ago Ron worked for a company that was rife with temptations. The owner hired receptionists and secretaries who were usually beautiful, young, and single; consequently, it was not a healthy environment for married men. In addition, some of Ron's male coworkers ate lunch at a "gentlemen's club"—a fancy term for a topless bar. They often asked Ron to go with them, and even though he was tempted, he never went. They'd try to entice him by saying, "We won't tell your wife. What she doesn't know won't hurt her." He would politely decline and say, "No thanks, I have a deal with my wife. I don't go to female strip clubs and she doesn't go to male strip clubs. They're dangerous places."

These coworkers all knew that Ron was a Christian, and if he'd gone, they would have discounted his faith and labeled him as a hypocrite. I know that several men admired Ron's commitment to me, because they privately asked for his advice about their marriages.

The best defense against an office affair is a healthy marriage. Your marriage could be an excellent example to other married coworkers if you stand strong. So be bold and fearless when you're defending your marriage.

### *In Your Home*

Your home should be a safe place. Make this verse your "power statement": "But as for me and my house, we will serve the LORD" (Josh. 24:15).

If you have a computer in your home, use it wisely. The Internet is amazing—and dangerous.

Donna would often sneak out of bed to "chat" with a man whom she met through a singles Web site. The fact that she wasn't single didn't seem to be relevant. When her husband, Larry, discovered his wife typing in the dark at 3:00 A.M., he confronted her. But she quickly logged off and denied any wrongdoing. After Donna left for work the next morning, he accessed the messages that she and her cyber-hunk had been sending. He read page after page of sexually explicit suggestions. Larry had no idea that his wife even knew such words! When he confronted her with the evidence, she came "clean" and said that she'd stop—but she didn't. She just became more secretive and better at hiding the evidence. Donna risked her marriage for a man she never met, and when Larry caught her again, he divorced her.

Internet pornography is one of the fastest growing cyber industries in the world, and it's been the cause of countless affairs and divorces. If Internet access is a problem for anyone in your family, apply the verse in Matthew 5:29: "If your . . . eye causes you to sin, pluck it out." And if your Internet access causes you to sin, plug it out! Keep the computer, but take it off-line. You and your family can still use it for word processing and playing computer games, but discontinuing your Internet service will fix the cyber-gap in your guarding hedge.

### *TV Temptations*

Cable television is another problem area in many homes. We recently signed up for digital cable TV with one month of free movie channels. The day after they hooked it up, I canceled all the movie channels because they all had X-rated movies. We don't allow pornography—in any form—in our home. We want to protect our son, Nick, and we want to protect ourselves, too.

Men are visual creatures, and they are naturally attracted to beautiful women wearing . . . nothing. If your husband has easy access to X-rated movies, he'll be tempted to watch them. Even strong Christian men can get caught in the "just one more" trap that ends in divorce. If your husband is comparing you to the eighteen-year-old hotties in porno movies, you will not, literally, measure up.

Jerry is a married Christian man who started getting up in the middle of the night to watch X-rated movie channels. The more he watched them, the more he wanted to watch. Eventually, the thoughts of his late-night "dates" with these beautiful willing-to-do-anything women consumed his life. He lost interest in his middle-aged wife, and when she caught him in his secret sin, he convinced her that it was her fault. She was ashamed to tell any of her friends or talk to their pastor, so she suffered in silence. He persuaded her to watch the movies with him, but it didn't solve their problems because she felt used, unloved, and dirty. He gave her his lust, but not his love.

The fatal venom of pornography poisoned their marriage.

### *Baby-sitter Blues*

Another important guarding hedge around your home involves your baby-sitters/nannies. Jayne and Dennis hired a lovely sixteen-year-old baby-sitter named Linda. But because they didn't have healthy guarding hedges in place, Linda is now married to Dennis!

Jayne didn't see the signs because it never occurred to her that her husband could ever be more than a fatherly mentor to "little Linda." After all, he was almost forty and she was just a child; it must be completely innocent. Wrong.

I invited Jayne, Dennis, and their kids to our anniversary party, and I thought it was odd that they brought their baby-sitter. Then, when Linda sat next to Dennis, I was a little more concerned. But when I saw him take several bites of food off the baby-sitter's plate, my Hedge Invasion Alarm System signaled a code red.

I told Jayne about my suspicions, and she told me that Dennis was just being extra nice to Linda because she was depressed about her parents' divorce. Jayne said, "We both love her. We think of her as our daughter."

A few months later, Dennis moved out. He married Linda as soon as she turned eighteen, and they now have two children of their own. I bet Linda won't let him drive *their* baby-sitter home.

My friend Renee always made sure that she was the one who picked up and dropped off the baby-sitter. Once, when she was unable to go, she sent all the kids with her husband. It's an excellent idea to have a third party ride along in those circumstances. Doing so is a protection for your husband, too, because he could be accused of something inappropriate. Even if he's innocent, it's his word against hers. Billy Graham has always been above reproach in these types of situations because he's never alone in a car with a woman, except his wife or daughters.

If you're in a financial position to have a nanny, I recommend an older Mrs. Doubtfire type. But even the actor who played her, Robin Williams, didn't follow that suggestion. He was married to Valerie for ten years, then he divorced his wife and married Marsha, his son's nanny.

A woman I met at Bible study had invited an underprivileged foreign exchange student to live in their home. The girl came with nothing and left with the woman's husband. When you let other people into your home, be very aware that problems like the ones above are a distinct possibility.

We have an extra bedroom in our house, and we live within walking distance of a college. We've considered the idea of renting the room to a student, but we can never agree on whom to rent to. Ron has in mind a twenty-ish female, Swedish blonde, massage-therapy student; I envision a male sun-kissed surfer, weightlifter, police academy cadet who'd help me vacuum. Since we can't agree, I guess we'll keep our guarding hedges in place.

### *At Church*

"Church?" you ask. Yes, church! I know of several marriages that were damaged by affairs that began at church. It usually begins innocently enough. Maybe both parties in the affair work with the youth group or start a Sunday school project, then, they look for more ways to work together—and play together. Christians who are married to non-Christians are especially vulnerable to this type of affair because they think, *If I were married to a Christian, I'd have a problem-free marriage.*

Another possible source of problems at church is pastoral counseling. Many women who have troubled marriages go to their pastor to get advice and encouragement, but sometimes the encouragement goes too far. Most churches have strict guidelines about pastors counseling women, because it's very easy for a healthy spiritual bond to turn into a dangerous emotional or physical connection.

Ron and I often talk to couples who are having marriage problems, and we're always on guard about any unhealthy connection that might begin. Once a troubled wife called the house and said, "I want to talk to Ron, alone."

I told her, "Sorry, we're a package deal. We only work as a team." She never called back.

### *For Your Hobbies*

My friend Annette is married to a man who loves to compete in the local drag races. She doesn't particularly care for cars or racing, but when she saw some of the "groupies" that hung around the racetrack, she decided to go with him every Saturday. It was a sacrifice on her part, but she's learned to enjoy it—except for the dirt, the noise, and the heat—because they do it together. She's a smart woman.

I always admired Paul McCartney's marriage to his late-wife Linda because she went on tour with him for almost thirty years. After all, he was a Beatle. She knew that women would be willing to do anything to "be" with Paul, so she set up a hedge around him—her! She usually brought the kids along too, and they were never apart for even one night—except for the time he was in jail for possession of marijuana. I didn't say he was a good role model in all areas.

Lance loved to ride bicycles, but his wife didn't. So he spent every Saturday on various cross-country rides, and she stayed in town. She often took the children to parks, movies, or birthday parties without him. Then he started riding on Sundays, too, and even some weekdays. His wife felt like he was more devoted to his bike than he was to her. She complained about his activities, but they never reached a compromise. When he met a beautiful woman cyclist who loved to ride as much as he did, he reached a "compromise" with *her,* if you get my drift.

If your hobby is a source of resentment, find a way to modify it where both of you will be happy and neither one of you will be unguarded.

Ron and I attended the wedding of a couple who met on a nightclub dance floor. They were both excellent dancers, and their whole lives were built around different clubs and dance contests. After they were married, Sandy was thrilled to have a home and wanted to settle into married life. She saw the club scene as part of their single life. She was willing to go dancing on Saturday night, but she would have preferred to make new "married couple" friends. He still wanted to dance—all weekend—so he started going out without her. And since he couldn't dance alone, he boogied with lots of pretty, single women.

I bet you can guess what happened. The hobby that they'd once shared became a fatal wedge in their marriage. If they'd found some way to satisfy both of their needs, they might have stayed together. Perhaps they could have found a couples' dance group or set aside one night for dancing and one night for making new married friends.

A Scottish proverb about compromise says, "It's better to bend, than break."

## SPIRITUAL GUARDING HEDGES

Just as you guard your marriage in physical ways, guard it in spiritual matters, too. Part of the reason our marriage nearly failed was our lack of spiritual discipline.

The *first* decision you must make as a couple is to find a strong Bible-based church and commit to regular attendance. If the church has midweek services, make every effort to attend them too, because they usually are a bit "deeper" than a Sunday morning service. Also, get involved in some other small-group activity such as home studies or a couples' Bible study. If you offer to help in a Sunday school class or as an usher, you'll feel like you're part of the group, make new "couple friends," and you'll feel like your church is your home away from home.

We've made an effort to become part of our church by attending the couples' Bible studies and retreats, working in the drama ministry, and serving as ushers. Every other month I attend to the needs of the new mothers in the "cry room." It's fun, because I get to hold screaming babies—one of my favorite sports.

The *second* spiritual guarding hedge is tithing. I know it's tough, but if you do it—give 10 percent—you'll be blessed beyond measure. My parents taught us the importance of this principle, and we can tell you from personal experience that the discipline of tithing will change your life. God doesn't need your money—He's not poor. But He knows that you need to give it. Holding on to money is like holding on to sand: if you try to grip it tightly in your fists, it will all run out. If, however, you hold your money in a giving position, hands together and palms up, you'll always have enough. Prayerfully discuss this with your spouse.

The *third* spiritual guarding hedge is consistency. If you want to be an example to your non-Christian friends, your walk had better match your talk. If you have children, remember, they're watching you. If you have dark secrets, bring them to the Light.

## PERSONALIZE YOUR GUARDING HEDGES

The key to growing effective guarding hedges is to be honest about your weaknesses, both as individuals and as a couple. Set up distinct boundaries and enforce them. If your spouse reminds you of the rules, don't be defensive or point out your spouse's faults; accept his or her correction because it's for the greater good of the marriage. Some of the most difficult phrases to say—*you're right* and *I'm sorry*—can save your marriage—and your love.

When Secret Service agents guard the president, they regard the president's life as more important than their own individual lives. Guard your marriages in the same way. You may be required to sacrifice part of your individual life—hobbies, profession, TV time, computer time, sports activities—to strengthen your marriage. If you're both willing to make your marriage a priority, however, and guard it from internal and external dangers, your home will be a safe haven.

---

### *Things to Think About*

1. Are there any weak spots in your guarding hedges? What about in your mate's hedges?
2. Does your walk match your talk? Are you the same person when no one is watching you?
3. What can you do to strengthen your spiritual hedges?

---

### *Things to Do*

1. Ask your mate, "Is there anything I'm doing that makes you feel uncomfortable, insecure, or suspicious?"
2. If your home is wired for the Internet, sign up for a family-friendly filter that will block all pornography. Get rid of any pornographic magazines, videos, and so forth, in your home.
3. Sit with your spouse and write out a code of conduct for your marriage. Include guidelines for your home, workplace, church, and hobbies.

Nine

# EDUCATING

*Dwell with [your wife/husband] according to knowledge.*

—I PETER 3:7 (KJV)

Late one evening, a woman from our church called. She asked if she and her husband could come over for some marriage advice. Twenty minutes later they sat on our sofa.

"What's up?" Ron asked.

Devin silently straightened the coasters on our coffee table. His wife, Colleen, said, "See, he won't even look at you. He just goes inside his shell and checks out. I want to talk about our problems, and he wants to ignore them . . . and me. We're so different. I don't understand him and he doesn't even try to understand me."

I asked Colleen, "How are you different?"

"Where do I start? He's a neat freak and I'm messy. He's an introverted couch potato who's addicted to the sports channel, and I love to have big parties for my friends and family. He grew up in a *Leave It to Beaver* style Christian home and my parents were hippies, so he thinks I was raised by wolves. We disagree about money and sex and tons of other things."

Ron turned to Devin and asked, "Are there any things you agree on?"

Devin rubbed his chin, picked at his fingernails, and mumbled, "We don't agree on much of anything. I have no idea what she wants from me. I was like this when she married me, but now she wants to change me."

Colleen interrupted him. "The things that attracted me to him were his quiet and calm personality and his ability to organize things. Now those same things drive me crazy! I'm not saying that I'm perfect, but I just want to have the kind of marriage my parents have—with lots of affection and laughter. I like to have fun and go with the flow, and he wants to analyze everything to death."

She bit her lip and looked at her shoes as she whispered, "Sometimes I feel like he doesn't care about me."

Devin took her hand and, without looking at her, said, "I do care about you . . . I just don't understand you."

Ron asked them, "Would you be willing to educate each other?"

They both nodded, and Ron said, "That willingness puts you way ahead of most couples. You've admitted that you have a problem and you've asked for help. You'll never fully understand each other, but if you're both prepared to study each other like a textbook, ask questions, and do your homework, you can get off each other's nerves and on each other's Dean's List."

Ron smiled and said, "Welcome to your first day of school!"

## IT'S A MATTER OF DEGREES

After earning their B.S., doctors study medicine for up to eight years before they earn an M.D. Attorneys study the intricacies of law for up to five years to get a J.D. Most women get their MRS. degree, however, without any education.

I was twenty-two when I got my MRS. degree and became Mrs. Ronald Anderson. Now, after twenty-six years, I'm still studying my husband because I want to get my PHD.

Let me explain: When God created man (Gen. 2:7), he saw that it was not good for Adam to be alone, so he created Eve to be Adam's helpmate. Eve did a really cruddy job, though; she got both of them in big-time trouble with God when she ate the forbidden fruit and gave it to Adam (vv. 16–17). She was designed to help him, but she chose to disobey God's instructions, and we women are still paying for it—through pain in childbirth (yeowwww!) and difficulties in our relationships with our husbands (double yeowww!).

I want to be a better helpmate than Eve was, so I'm obeying God's command in 1 Peter 3:7: "Dwell with [your husband/wife] according to knowledge" (KJV). I'm acquiring knowledge about Ron in order to get my PHD (Professional Helpmate Degree).

There are four main areas of study:

1. the differences between men and women;
2. the differences in personalities;
3. the differences in family backgrounds;
4. our own individual differences.

You'll be required to study each of these categories until you fully understand your mate. In other words, you'll never be done.

**Note to husbands:** If you're reading this book as a couple, you may also study these same courses to get your PHD (Perceptive Husband Degree).

## AREA 1: DIFFERENCES BETWEEN MEN AND WOMEN

*Why can't a woman be more like a man?*[1]

—PROFESSOR HENRY HIGGINS

*MY FAIR LADY*

Genetically speaking, females have two X chromosomes, and males have one X and one Y chromosome. The difference is in the Y, but I think it should be spelled "*Why?*" because that's the way we begin most of the questions we ask each other. "*Why* do you cry all the time? What's wrong with you?" asks the man. The woman replies, "*Why* don't you *ever* cry? What's wrong with *you*?"

God created us to work as a team, so some of the strengths of men compliment the weaknesses of women and vice versa. If you could mix us together in a blender without pureeing us, we'd make one heck of a wonderful person. The fabulous thing about male-female relationships is that we can help balance each other out; the not so fabulous part is that we can drive each other insane.

Women are in general more emotional, and men generally tend

to be more logical. Ron is an accountant, so he likes columns of numbers to add up and balance, but I've always been more of an estimator. Ron will "work" his way through a problem by making a game plan and setting goals, and I'll "feel" my way through it by talking it to death, asking for twenty-five opinions, and buying in to worry like it was on the half-price rack.

Men are usually single-task oriented and women can mega-multitask. Picture the wife: She's talking on the phone, stirring the spaghetti sauce, bouncing a baby on her hip, balancing her checkbook, and analyzing why her older sister looks younger than she does—all at the same time.

Meanwhile, the husband is reading the newspaper—period. I don't know if you ladies have caught on to this, but when a man's reading the newspaper, that's all he can do. If you don't believe me, the next time he's reading the sports page ask him a two-part question like, "What's your favorite place in the whole wide world and why?" He won't be able to answer you without putting down the paper. Try it—it's funny.

Most couples we've talked to think the biggest difference between men and women is how they think and feel about sex. Sex is, in fact, such a huge factor in most extramarital affairs, that topic will be explored fully in the next chapter, titled "Satisfying." For now, though, let's stick to the differences in how often men and women think about "it." If men are awake, they're thinking about it, and if men are asleep, they're dreaming about it. Contrast those 24/7 thought waves with the typical woman, who's probably only thinking about it while she's doing it. And sometimes, not even then.

Men see life through sex-colored glasses. I'm always surprised at the way men hear sexual overtones in nonsexual conversations. The other day Ron and I were standing in the kitchen making our plans for the day, and I matter-of-factly said, "I need to balance the checkbook." He immediately got "that look" on his face, slithered over to me, rubbed my shoulders, and purred, "I'd love to balance *your* checkbook!"

I have to be careful when I put any verb and noun together indicating a task. For example, I avoid phrases like "I need to turn on the porch light," because he'll wink at me and say, "I'll turn on *your* porch light!"

Another difference is that women are often more sensitive than men, and that can be a huge source of conflict. If a woman is frequently told, "Lighten up! Don't be so sensitive!" she'll either stop expressing her feelings and pull away, or she'll toughen up. If she stops being sensitive, then he'll probably complain, "Hey, you're just like one of the guys; act like a lady!" God designed women to be soft, sensitive, and nurturing. Those qualities help us to be great mothers.

There are hundreds of physical, mental, and spiritual differences between men and women. If these are a source of conflict or confusion in your marriage, I hope you'll both continue to study, understand, and appreciate your differences.

For further study in each area, see the list of recommended reading at the end of this chapter.

## AREA 2: DIFFERENCES IN PERSONALITIES

*I'm just a shy guy, wish I was a sly guy.*

—NAT KING COLE
*I'M A SHY GUY*[2]

Ron is an outgoing optimist. And—can you believe it—that's not illegal. He's the life of every party. He's never met a stranger, and he assumes that everyone likes him—and they do! He once saw a grubby old homeless man eating alone at a coffee shop, so Ron approached him and asked, "Mind if I join you?" They had a great conversation, and Ron thought the old guy was fascinating.

In high school, Ron was voted "Friendliest Senior" and "Funniest Senior."

On the other hand, I could have been voted "Most Likely to Eat Lunch Alone." I was a shy, lonely pessimist. I assumed from the get-go that no one wanted to talk to me. If they did, I thought it was because they felt sorry for me or wanted to get some info about me so they could laugh at me behind my back. My dearest wish—to be invisible.

I don't feel that way anymore, though, because I decided that I was missing out on too many wonderful experiences. I wanted to develop skills to become friendlier, so I studied Ron and other extroverts and learned how to put on my "happy hat." I listened, watched, and practiced. The more I forced myself to be friendly, stopped thinking about myself, and tried to see the bright side of things, the easier it got. I've learned to take more risks because I know that I won't die—even if I do say something stupid. (Not that I ever have.)

I've even helped other people overcome their natural shyness and insecurities with a method I've developed—along with my friend Tonya Ruiz—called the TALK method of communication. We hope to publish a book about it soon.

We all have different personalities, so it's helpful to learn as much as we can about our mate's personalities and our own. Our natural traits don't, however, give us an excuse for rude, negative, or self-destructive behavior. As Christians, we should all have the same ultimate goal concerning our attitudes and behavior: "Only let your conduct be worthy of the gospel of Christ" (Phil. 1:27).

Ron and I started our marriage with opposite personalities, but we've both changed a lot. He's helped me to be more confident and joyful, and I've taught him to be more sensitive and patient. Because we understand each other, we no longer resent each other's personalities; we've learned to work as a team.

## AREA 3: DIFFERENCES IN FAMILY BACKGROUNDS

*Well, I was raised a coal miner's daughter.*

—LORETTA LYNN
*COAL MINER'S DAUGHTER*[3]

Peter and Cathy had just spent their first night in their new home after their honeymoon. Peter was a morning person and Cathy had warned him, "I don't do mornings." But he thought that if he made her a delicious breakfast with bacon, eggs, buttered toast, and fresh-ground coffee, she'd be thrilled. He thought that she would joyfully jump out of bed, eat her hearty breakfast, listen to him read the newspaper to her, take a quick shower, and plan their day.

That's the way his parents always started *their* day, so that's how it should be done.

Cathy didn't see it that way. She liked to take a bath at night and sleep as long as possible in the morning. The smell of fried eggs made her sick to her stomach, and the only time she read a newspaper was when she was looking for a new job or a lost kitten. Cathy grew up with a family of vagabond night owls who rarely ate meals together and seldom planned anything.

When Peter strutted into their bedroom with a lumberjack breakfast and a rose on a silver tray, he thought, *This should show her how much I love her.* He gently sang, "Hon-neee waaake uuup."

She burrowed deeper under the quilt and made a bovine grunting noise.

He was shocked. He thought, *Perhaps she didn't hear me.* He opened the drapes so she could see what a beautiful, sunny day it was.

She moaned like a dying dinosaur.

*Perhaps she's ill.* He pulled down the quilt; she pulled it up over her head and barked, "Why must you torture me? Go away!"

Peter ate his breakfast—alone and bewildered.

They were married, but they didn't know each other. Neither approach to morning was right or wrong—just different. Peter eventually learned to let a sleeping dog . . . um, wife . . . lie while he silently popped out of bed. He always opened the window as he cooked his eggs and quietly read his paper aloud—to the cat.

When Cathy eventually stumbled into the kitchen, she tried her best to be pleasant as she let him bring her a cup of coffee. They never saw eye-to-eye on mornings, but once they learned what the other person needed, they found a way to meet in the middle.

Have you ever asked your mate, "Why do you do it *that* way?" If you have, you probably got this answer: "Because that's the way my family's always done it."

Our families of origin have a huge impact on our behavior as adults. If the husband was poor and the wife was Daddy's Little Princess, the couple will probably have conflicts over money. If both the husband's and the wife's parents were divorced, the couple will be more likely to consider divorce as a solution to their problems.

Ron and I have very different backgrounds. I grew up in a small Midwestern town, where I lived in a two-story home with a big yard, a perfect apple tree, and a custom-built swing set. Ron spent his early years in the not-so-nice neighborhoods of various cities where he lived with his family, all seven of them, in tiny apartments. All those things in our backgrounds affect the way we act and react to each other and the world.

The key to resolving the differences in your families' backgrounds is understanding them. So ask each other about childhood experiences; try to duplicate the best parts and bring comfort and healing to the worst parts.

## AREA 4: INDIVIDUAL DIFFERENCES

*You like potatoes. And I like po-tah-toes*
*You like tomatoes. And I like to-mah-toes*
*Potatoes, po-tah-toes, tomatoes, to-mah-toes*
*Let's call the whole thing off.*

—IRA GERSHWIN
*LET'S CALL THE WHOLE THING OFF*[4]

One Saturday afternoon, Ron was happily watching a football game, but I was in the mood to be outside. So I spent two hours washing and waxing his new red sedan. It looked wonderful, and I was very proud of myself. I thought, *I'm the greatest wife in the world!*

When the game was over, I excitedly told him, "I have a wonderful surprise for you. Follow me!" As we walked out to the driveway, I pointed to the car and boasted, "I washed it *and* waxed it! Isn't it beautiful?"

His face froze, as he said, "Why did you do *that?* The windows are all streaked. Besides, I *like* to go to the car wash."

I planted my hands on my hips and said, "I did something nice for you . . . gave you a gift . . . and you just spit on it! My old boyfriend Mike was always thrilled when I washed *his* car!"

"Well, I'm not Mike, am I? I don't want you to wash my car. If you want to do something to please me, wash some dirty clothes. The laundry pile is big enough to ski on!"

"*That* would make you happy?"

"I'd be thrilled! That pile drives me nuts!"

I was shocked. "I had no idea that dirty laundry bothered you. It's never bothered me."

"Obviously."

That day, I asked him to make a list of the things that were important to him. It was an amazing revelation. I made a list too, and when he started doing the things on my list, I was elated. Over the years, we've reworked it and put a positive spin on it by calling it a love list.

When we speak to couples' groups, we give them a sheet of paper and tell them to write down the top five things that their spouse can do to please them. You'd be surprised at some of the things on their lists . . . or maybe you wouldn't. The man typically includes "have more sex," but we rarely see that request on a woman's list. The woman's list usually includes "talk to me more," but I've never seen that on a man's list.

The requests most likely to be honored are those that are both specific and doable. For example, "be more romantic" is too vague; that could mean different things to different people. "Bring me flowers once a month" or "kiss me good-bye every morning" would be more specific. Also, your request must be doable. Don't ask your wife to "look like a super model" or "keep the house clean *all* the time." Instead, you could write, "wear a dress for our date night" or "make the bed in the morning." If your requests are reasonable and realistic, your mate will be more likely to honor them.

One of the things on my list is "wait for me while I'm getting out of the car." In the early years, when we'd arrive at our destination, he'd be inside before I had time to round up my purse, find my keys, check my lipstick, and lock the car. I explained, "I feel abandoned when you leave me. I want to walk in—together." Once he knew that was a big deal, he got much better at waiting. His willingness to please me made me want to please him, too.

## BENEFITS OF YOUR PHD

Study your mate as if he or she is a textbook and you are studying for a final exam. If we make an effort to learn about our mates' preferences and priorities, they'll feel understood and appreciated. If we educate ourselves about the various differences between us and our mates, and work on ways to play to each others' strengths, we'll build strong hedges around our marriages.

## Things to Think About

1. What are the biggest differences between my mate and me?
2. Have I been studying my mate in order to understand—or to change—him or her?
3. What are some things I wish my spouse understood about me?

## Things to Do

1. Make your "I feel loved when you/we ______" list. List at least three specific things. Some examples: have sex twice a week, pray together every morning, compliment me, drive slower, iron my shirts, attend church together, make sure clean towels are in the bathroom, help me give the kids a bath. Remember, there are no right or wrong answers. If it's important to you—it's important!
2. Ask your mate to make his or her list. Then *do* the number one thing on that list without complaining, defending your past behavior, or saying how stupid it is—even if it is.
3. Carry your mate's list with you and, during this next week, do as many things as possible.
4. Compliment and thank your mate when he or she does something on your list.
5. Continue to update your lists as new needs arise. Keep doing this until you die.

## Recommended Reading

I'll never fully grasp how a man sees the world, but I've been able to get a handle on it by reading dozens of books on the subject. Most of those books were as dry as low-carb toast, but I found a great one that's funny, informative, and written from a Christian point of view.

Farrell, Bill and Pam. *Men Are Like Waffles and Women Are Like Spaghetti.* Eugene, Ore.: Harvest House, 2001.

Here's an excellent book for understanding how your different personalities affect your marriage.

Littauer, Florence. *Personality Plus for Couples: Understanding Yourself and the One You Love.* Old Tappan, N.J.: Revell, 2001.

For a fun book about marriage, this is a lighthearted look at the differences between what we *thought* we were getting and what we actually got!

Walker, Laura Jensen. *Dated Jekyll, Married Hyde: Or, Whatever Happened to Prince Charming?* Old Tappan, N.J.: Revell, 2003.

If sexual compatibility is a problem, here is a helpful book for women who want to feel more "in the mood."

Gregoire, Sheila Wray. *Honey, I Don't Have a Headache Tonight: Help for Women Who Want to Feel More "In the Mood."* Grand Rapids: Kregel, 2004.

Ten

# SATISFYING

*You will be like a well-watered garden.*

—ISAIAH 58:11 (NIV)

Don and Paula knew everything there was to know about having a healthy marriage. They attended an excellent Bible-based church for Sunday and Wednesday services, and went to couples' retreats and Bible studies.

Paula knew what her husband's needs were, and he knew what was important to her, so they worked hard to please each other. Then they both got too busy with work, children's activities, and life. They started to drift apart. The more they drifted, the more they resented each other. Don wasn't as romantic as he used to be, and Paula started to be "unavailable" when he wanted to make love. They both noticed the changes, but neither of them did anything to resolve their differences, so the gap widened. They continued their marriage, but they lived without passion or pleasure—as though they were only business partners.

Then Paula met Keith. He thrilled her beyond words. He was everything Don used to be. She selfishly followed her feelings. Instead of resolving the problems with her husband, she filed for divorce and told Don, "I just don't love you anymore."

All of their knowledge about each other turned out to be worthless. They knew what to do; they just didn't want to do it. The Bible warns us, "But be doers of the word, and not hearers only, deceiving yourselves" (James 1:22). Knowledge without action, then, is useless. Instead of choosing to obey God's Word, Don and Paula chose to satisfy their own needs over those of their mate. That selfishness killed their marriage.

## GOT WATER?

A well-watered plant will have roots that grow deep and strong, and it will be content to stay in its own garden. But a plant that is thirsting for water will send its roots out in search of quenching, perhaps going outside its hedges. Or it may be so starved that it drinks toxic water. If your spouse is well-watered, however, then your home and your marriage garden will be satisfying—for both of you.

Metaphorically speaking, if the husband waters the wife and the wife waters the husband, they will both be satisfied. "Drink water from your own well—share your love only with your wife [husband]" (Prov. 5:15 NLT).

Most men have affairs because of unmet physical, sexual needs; most women have affairs because of unsatisfied emotional needs for affection and tenderness. The root of unfaithfulness, however, is the desire for intimacy. Women usually long for emotional, affectionate intimacy, and most men want physical, sexual intimacy. These needs overlap, of course, and many people go outside their hedges for both emotional *and* sexual reasons.

## A MAN OR A MONSTER?

Long before I'd done any research on the subject, I noticed that Ron's need for sexual contact was much stronger than mine. On the days when we made love, he was mellow and easygoing about things that might normally have bothered him—like a mountain of laundry. During the day after, he was still patient, kind, and cuddly as a six-foot teddy bear. On the third day after our session, he would start to get restless and make sarcastic comments like, "Don't worry about me. You just live your life and I'll wait here."

Then, if we hadn't played doctor in four days, the veins in his eyes would get red and bulgy and his upper lip would start to twitch. If we went into the fifth day, he'd start to gnaw on the sofa.

The longer he went without release, the more pressurized—that is, grumpy—he became. If we ever went a whole week without sex, his skin would turn green, black bolts would pop out of his neck, and he would morph into Franken-Husband. My initial research wasn't clinical, just anecdotal. I saw a pattern: the longer he went without sex, the more irritable he became. Ladies, if you aren't "taking care of business" once or twice a week, you may be creating your own monster.

Ron and I talked about my theory, and he agreed with it. He said, "After several days without sex, I start to resent you and feel like you don't care about me. It isn't a conscious decision, but my resentment just starts to build and keeps getting worse each day that you ignore or reject me."

## MEN'S NUMBER-ONE NEED

Then actual research confirmed our experience. Men's need for sexual release is based on actual physical, hormonal needs. Many studies agree that because of sperm production, natural testosterone, and other factors, men naturally want sexual release about every seventy-two hours, or three days.

Men need sexual contact. It's not bad or dirty or perverted, it just *is.* If a wife makes an effort to meet her husband's needs, he'll be more willing to meet hers.

**Note:** All humans are unique and you may not list sex or affection as your number-one need, but I'll bet they're in your top three. According to *His Needs, Her Needs* by Willard F. Harley Jr., such is usually the case. He writes, "Sadly enough, most affairs start because of a lack of affection (for the wife) and a lack of sex (for the husband). It's a vicious cycle. She doesn't get enough affection, so she shuts him off sexually. He doesn't get enough sex, so the last thing he feels like being is affectionate."[1]

Sex is number one on Ron's list and approximately number forty-seven on mine, but I honor its importance to him.

### *You Are Sex-Driving Me Crazy!*

I don't fully understand the hormonal, physical male sex drive, but I do know a thing or two about the female hormone cycles. Ladies, have you ever gone on a PMS-driven mission called "Gotta have chocolate, or someone's gonna die"? I have. I once ransacked every drawer in my son's room looking for last year's semisweet Easter bunny's ear.

I've clawed through the kitchen cupboards like Indiana Jones on a quest, looking for a little golden bag containing stale chocolate chips. As I ripped it open and blissfully inhaled the aroma, my pulse reacted as if I'd just found the necklace that the old lady threw off the Titanic.

Now imagine that you're on a take-no-prisoners chocolate chase and your husband has a Snickers bar in his locked briefcase—but he won't give you the key. He has the capability to relieve your hormonal obsession, but he refuses. How would you feel about him? Would you think that he was selfish? Mean? Cruel?

Ron says that's how a man feels when his wife rejects his sexual needs.

### *Would You Like a Me-Burger?*

If you think of a man's sexual need as a hunger, his desire can be satisfied in many different ways. Each "feeding" does not have to be a banquet. His wife could "feed the need" with a snack, a meal, or a feast.

Often, a quick snack will satisfy his appetite. Other times, he'll be thrilled to sit down (lie down) for a simple meal. On special occasions, however, get out the good china (satin sheets), send the kidlettes to Grandma's house, and flambé a fabulous feast.

Ladies, next time your husband gets hungry for you and you're too tired to prepare a banquet, ask him, "How about a quick snack?" He'll probably be thrilled that you're not rejecting him, and you'll be able to meet his need without resenting it.

## *Don't Make Him Beg*

Bambi had four children in five years. She went from being a sex kitten to a fat cat who craved catnaps. She lost all interest in sex and was so tired that she had a "headache" for most of the next decade. When her husband tried to get frisky, she'd often arch her back and hiss, "You must be kidding!" He wasn't. She refused him so many times that he quit asking. Not surprisingly, they're now divorced and in the middle of a bitter custody battle over the kittens.

Men have fragile egos in this area and, in order to avoid rejection, they may stop pursuing their wives.

Ladies, if your husband isn't asking anymore, immediately sprint into a lingerie shop. I mean now, this minute! Put down the book, march in there, and buy a little—and I mean *little*—something. Then call your hubby and say, "I'm cookin' up somethin' special for dinner—hurry home!"

Unless your husband is a eunuch, he has sexual needs. Do your best to satisfy them.

## *"But I'm Embarrassed"*

I don't know why, but men are stimulated by visual cues. That's why they're much more likely to look at pornography than women are.

That's also why they like to make love with the lights on. I'd prefer the flattering glow of a single votive candle, but Ron wants to use the same wattage a dentist uses for a root canal. So we have a conflict.

My body is almost fifty years old, and it's showing signs of wear. I think of it as a comfy sofa: lumpy, frayed, and a little saggy. I try to avoid full-length mirrors, but my hubby still wants to see me—and that's a good thing.

Several years ago, we discovered a wonderful compromise: we use a red light bulb in the lamp next to our bed. I know it sounds crazy, but don't knock it until you've tried it. The pinkish glow diminishes most flaws, wrinkles, and stretch marks. You can buy these magic bulbs at most larger grocery stores for less than five dollars. The one I get is called a GE 25 Watt Crystal Color Party Light. Party hearty!

In a well-watered relationship, each person receives what he or she needs. Some couples, though, need a water gauge to determine how their plant's roots are doing. Ideally, you should be at a place in your marriage where you can ask each other, "Are you happy with our sex life?" If one of you is not, ask, "Why not?" As a married couple, it's vital that you are able to discuss your needs openly and honestly. If it's important to one of you, it needs to be important to both of you.

If you're having major conflicts in this area, an excellent book to read together is *Intended for Pleasure: Sex Technique and Sexual Fulfillment in Christian Marriage* by Ed Wheat and Gaye Wheat.[2]

## WOMEN'S NUMBER-ONE NEED

Again, one of the most important needs for many women is affection. That's why many women love to read tender and dreamy romance novels and enjoy romantic "chick flick" movies. Most women think that the ideal man would cherish her more than his car and be willing to throw himself in front of a speeding garbage truck to save her from harm.

The men in the romantic books and movies never have bad hair days or acid indigestion, and they always smell like suntan lotion or better yet . . . cookies. If such a Harlequin Harry exists, I've never met him, so I'll be content with my Regular Ron.

I love it when Ron calls me from work just to tell me that he misses me. I feel special when he stops on his way home to buy me my favorite candy bar—Snickers (in case you want to get me something for my birthday).

When Ron and I were first married, though, he didn't do any of the things that made me feel special. He was only affectionate when he wanted something from me. This lack of attention and affection from Ron was the reason I became attracted to Jake. While we were having our affair, Jake noticed what I wore and complimented me when I changed my hairstyle or got a new piece of jewelry. He was always tender and affectionate. He'd hurry to open a door for me and always asked my opinion.

He was meeting my needs, but not his wife's. I realize now that he was a lousy husband to her, and he probably would have been a terrible husband to me if we'd married.

When Ron and I started to rebuild our marriage, he worked hard to please me. Even though he didn't do everything I wanted, I complimented him when I saw that he was trying.

Men, if you want your wife to be content and fulfilled in your relationship, be affectionate, considerate, and gentle. If your wife sees that you're trying to meet her needs, she'll feel secure, safe, and satisfied in your arms.

## WHY ME?

You might be thinking, *Why should I be the first to change?* or *How come I have to do all the work?* The answer is simple: God will work with whomever is available and give that person the strength to change. Be available.

You already know that you can't change your mate, but you can change your own behavior. The word *change* indicates a transformation, which is a metamorphosis; the word *metamorphosis* begins with the two letters *me.* Change begins with *me.*

If you want a vibrant and loving marriage, make this verse your prayer: "Create in *me* a clean heart, O God, and renew a steadfast spirit within *me*" (Ps. 51:10).

## CAN'T GET NO SATISFACTION

If either you or your spouse constantly hums the Rolling Stones' tune, "I Can't Get No Satisfaction," you might be in trouble. If you ignore each other's needs, one or both of you will be more tempted to seek affection/sex elsewhere. Not having needs met is no excuse, of course, for bad behavior, and going after sex outside of your marriage is sin; the Bible says—to *both* of you—be satisfied with the wife/husband of your youth (Prov. 5:18; Mal. 2:15). That verse indicates that we should be trying not only to remain satisfied with our mates, but should be satisfying each other's needs. If your marriage is well-watered, the grass on the other side of the fence will not look greener than your own. And if you're both content and secure in your marriage, the Flirty Franks and Teasing Tinas at the office won't be as tempting.

Maybe you're saying, "But, Nancy, you don't know *my* husband/ wife." If you married that person, you must have picked him or her. So unless your spouse is dangerous or a threat to your children, you can choose to be satisfied. Look for the best in your mate, not at his or her faults. The more you meet your spouse's needs, the more he or she will meet yours. It doesn't matter who plants the seeds first, because you'll enjoy the harvest—together. It might be hard to start, but if you don't, and your mate won't, then who will?

It's easy to get complacent and just continue doing what you've always done. Since nothing ever stays the same, small changes can sneak up on us and cause some big problems.

Ron recently had a conversation with his sixty-year-old friend Earl. Earl said, "For years, my feet have been killing me. I bought insole cushions for my shoes and even bought an expensive pair of arch supports, but nothing helped. So I finally went to a podiatrist."

"What did he say?" Ron asked.

"He X-rayed my feet. After he looked at the films, he asked, 'What size shoe do you wear?' I answered, 'Eleven.' Then the doctor said, 'No wonder your feet hurt, you should wear a size thirteen!'"

Earl shook his head and told Ron, "I've been buying size eleven shoes since high school. It never occurred to me to measure my feet to see if they'd grown."

His shoes have been too small for decades! His feet had changed, but he wasn't paying attention.

Have you measured your marriage lately?

## GROWING PAINS

If you're struggling in your relationship and feel like you've grown apart from your spouse, today can be the day of new beginnings. I know how lonely, desperate, and exhausted you may feel, because I've felt that way. Do you remember how bad our marriage was in the beginning of this book? We were both selfish and angry; we aren't anymore, however. Well . . . I'm still a little selfish, but mostly our lives are full of light and love—and yours can be too.

Fighting and blaming won't work. Commanding and demanding can't work. Surrender works. If you surrender your heart to the Lord, and ask Him to work *in* you and *through* you, He will accomplish more than you could ever do on your own.

Ron and I still don't agree on all issues, but we've surrendered or reached a compromise on most of the major ones; the minor ones, then—like which way the toilet paper should hang on the dispenser—won't break us. We've learned to work together as a team, and that is our prayer for you. You already know what you need to do. Now have fun doing it!

> And let us not grow weary while doing good, for in due season we shall reap if we do not lose heart. (Galatians 6:9)

> It seems to me that love, if fine, is essentially a discipline.
>
> —W. B. YEATS

---

## Things to Think About

1. Are you happy with your sex life? If not, what would you like to change?
2. Have emotional barriers—resentment, unforgiveness, jealousy, anger—come between you? How can you overcome them?
3. Do you know your mate's "shoe size"? Not his or her literal one, but your spouse's emotional one. How has your spouse changed over the years of your marriage? Did you notice and adjust to those changes?

---

## Things to Do

1. Read about the perils of adultery in Proverbs 5 and 6.
2. Go buy a red light bulb.

3. Pray together and ask God to be your marriage counselor. Surrender to His will for your lives, and do not grow weary of pleasing each other.

# Conclusion

Now that you've read the whole book—you didn't skip the Bible verses, did you?—you have all the information you need to plant, water, and feed the six new hedges around your marriage.

Applying this information can make your home a tranquil oasis and help you rediscover the wonderful qualities that originally attracted you to each other.

Within the shelter of your hedges, you can have a beautiful, fragrant garden filled with love and laughter, and overflowing with Living Water.

*Please make a copy of the outline on the following page and put it where you will see it—and do it—every day.*

*Happy Hedging!*

## THE CONCEPT OF HEDGES

HEDGES will protect your marriage from the intrusion of external temptations as well as provide internal support structures, keeping the bad things out and the good things in!

> A man planted a vineyard and set a hedge around it. (Mark 12:1)

### *Hearing*

Listen to each other with your ears *and* with your hearts. Install a filter between your brain and your mouth, and censor cruel and angry words.

> The hearing ear and the seeing eye,
> The LORD has made both of them. (Proverbs 20:12)

### *Encouraging*

Help your mate with your hands, ears, lips, and prayers. Create a cycle of praise. Rediscover the power of a compliment.

> So then, let us aim for harmony . . . and try to build each other up. (Romans 14:19 NLT)

### *Dating*

Enjoy each other. Explore ways to keep romance, surprise, and excitement alive in your relationship. Create a life that celebrates marriage.

> Let your fountain be blessed, And rejoice with the wife [husband] of your youth. (Proverbs 5:18)

### *Guarding*

Establish rules for your relationship. Set clearly defined boundaries that neither of you is allowed to change without mutual agreement.

> Above all else, guard your heart, for it affects everything you do. (Proverbs 4:23 NLT)

### *Educating*

Study your mate. Become an expert. Learn what you can do to please him or her. Have your spouse write a "wish list" for your relationship.

> Dwell with [your wife/husband] according to knowledge. (1 Peter 3:7a KJV)

### *Satisfying*

Meet the needs of your spouse. Once you know what to do, just do it. Make it an adventure to form new need-meeting habits. If your mate is "well-watered" at home, he or she will be satisfied to stay on *your* side of the fence.

> You will be like a well-watered garden. (Isaiah 58:11 NIV)

* * * *

If you would like more information about Nancy, want to order an audio CD of *The Death and Resurrection of Our Marriage,* would like to inquire about Ron and Nancy speaking at your couples' group, or would like Nancy to speak to your women's group, go to her Web site at www.NancyCAnderson.com.

# Endnotes

*Chapter 2: Confession*

1. Exodus 20:2–3; Deuteronomy 5:6–7
2. Ephesians 6:1
3. Proverbs 14:1
4. 1 John 1:9
5. John 8:11b

*Chapter 6: Encouraging*

1. Florence Littauer, *After Every Wedding Comes a Marriage* (Eugene, Ore.: Harvest House, 1997).

*Chapter 7: Dating*

1. *The Christian Bed and Breakfast Directory* (Uhrichsville, Ohio: Barbour, 2002).

*Chapter 8: Guarding*

1. "Workplace a Hazard to Marriage," *Orange County Register,* 24 November 2003.

*Chapter 9: Educating*

1. From "A Hymn to Him" by Alan Jay Lerner, 1956.
2. From "I'm a Shy Guy" by Nathaniel Cole, © Decca Records, date unavailable.
3. From "Coal Miner's Daughter" by Loretta Lynn, © Sure Fire Music, Inc., 1970.

4. From "Let's Call the Whole Thing Off" by Ira Gershwin, 1937.

*Chapter 10: Satisfying*

1. Willard F. Harley Jr., *His Needs, Her Needs* (Old Tappan, N.J.: Revell, 1986), 43.
2. Ed Wheat and Gaye Wheat, *Intended for Pleasure: Sex Technique and Sexual Fulfillment in Christian Marriage,* 3d ed. (Grand Rapids: Revell, 1997).